The Long Road

The Long Road

A Memoir

by
Aubrey Lewis Brown
1911–1990

Sable Press
Calgary

D. H. Brown
Sable Press Canada
sablepress@telus.net

Library and Archives Canada Cataloguing in Publication

The Long Road : The winding journey of faith that led Aubrey Brown from rural Australia, through the jungles of the Congo to the foothills of the Rocky Mountains.

Brown, Aubrey Lewis, author

Brown, Aubrey, 1911-1992. 2. Missionaries - Democratic Republic of Congo – Biography. 3. WEC International – Biography. 4. DR Congo - History - Civil War 1960-1965 - Personal Narratives.

Paperback ISBN 978-0-9699911-2-0
Hardcover ISBN 978-0-9699911-3-7
Content ID: 23358469

Book design by Alexis Tjart
Cover by Melina Cusano and Dave Brown
Original map, italicized editorial comments, 1986 author's portrait and epilogue by Dave Brown
First Edition, June 2019
Printed and distributed by Lulu Publishing

On-line WordPress blog version - April, 2017
(aubreysbistro.wordpress.com)
Blog edited and additional content by Ron Brown and Dave Brown
Blog version design and image preparation by Dave Brown

Table of Contents

FOREWORD VII

PROLOGUE IX

CHAPTER 1 EARLY LIFE 1911 TO 1935 1

BEGINNINGS 3

PRESCHOOL YEARS 5

SCHOOL DAYS 9

FARMING 10

CONVERSION 15

TEEN YEARS 17

THE CALL 19

CHAPTER 2 TRAINING 1935 TO 1939 21

MELBOURNE BIBLE INSTITUTE 23

FROM MELBOURNE TO LONDON 27

MISSIONARY TRAINING IN ENGLAND 35

LANGUAGE SCHOOL IN FRANCE 43

CHAPTER 3 FIRST TERM 1940 TO 1950 49

IBAMBI 51

THREE TREKS AND LUBUTU 55

KONDOLOLE AND NIANGARA 69

THE MOVE TO NALA AND THE WEDDING 69

CHAPTER 4 FIRST FURLOUGH 1951 TO 1952 85

AUSTRALIA AND CANADA 87

CHAPTER 5 SECOND TERM 1953 TO 1959 97

OPIENGE 99

CHAPTER 6 SECOND FURLOUGH 1960 TO 1962 111

CANADA AND AUSTRALIA 113

CHAPTER 7 THIRD TERM 1962 TO 1964 121

POKO 123

REBELS, PRISON AND RESCUE 127

CHAPTER 8 THIRD FURLOUGH 1965 TO 1971 139

CANADA 141

CHAPTER 9 FOURTH TERM 1971 TO 1975 155

POKO AND MULITA 157

CHAPTER 10 RETIREMENT IN CANADA 1975 TO 1989 175

1975 TO 1989 177

EPILOGUE, 1989 TO 1992 197

Foreword

In 1987, Dad was 76 years of age and living in Three Hills, Alberta, Canada.

I was 38 years of age living in Africa and raising two young daughters.

I wanted them to know their grandfather, to know that in his generation he loved God and served Him by making a difference in Africa. I desired this also for his numerous grandchildren and the succeeding generations yet to come.

I knew that Dad had returned from Australia, after his last sibling died, with a shoe box filled with the letters he had written to his mother during his Africa years, including dozens of family photographs. I suggested he spend the next couple of winters going through those letters and writing up the story of his life, a life lived on three continents.

By the spring of 1990, two years before his death, his carefully handwritten autobiography was complete. It basically followed the format of his letters home, a kind of diary with highlights of each year and term. Using the letters as primary sources he wrote from memory.

As I read his story, my eyes often filled with tears as I understood more of the loneliness and hardships he had faced. Yet I was also struck by how often he said he was so happy with his life in Africa. His heart's desire was to see spiritually lost people in Africa come to know Jesus and to that end he walked and biked to some of the most remote villages just to bring the good news of Jesus. He was the first white man many children had seen. He was Jesus to them.

Today his three remaining children remember him as a quiet, godly man with a single, determined passion to faithfully finish his journey on that long road that wound from Australia, through the Congo, to Canada.

Ron Brown
Calgary, June 2014

Prologue

Aubrey Brown left his family farm in Victoria, Australia and worked for over thirty-five years in what is now the Democratic Republic of Congo. There he met his Canadian wife and together they raised four children. He held many positions within a Protestant inter-denominational mission group: church planting in remote areas, teaching in primary schools, helping adult students up-grade academic skills in preparation for Bible School, teaching in those Bible Schools, and representing the mission in speaking tours throughout both Canada and Australia. This would be in addition to the more mundane but necessary tasks involved in living and working in a developing country: building, maintaining and repairing mission buildings, overseeing work crews, purchasing and transporting supplies, ferrying in-coming and out-going mission staff between often remote mission stations and transportation hubs, regularly corresponding with family and supporting churches, as well as helping to raise a family. Above all, Aubrey cultivated and maintained relationships with the people he lived and worked with, regardless of skin colour.

He and his wife Hulda, retired in Alberta, where in those later Canadian years, the Three Hills home became a base for their children as they came and went to various African countries or other parts of Canada in the course of their careers.

The text is as Aubrey wrote it out by hand twenty-five years ago, although a few of his very short sentences were joined together and some awkward phrasing changed to allow the text to have increased clarity and flow. I've occasionally added footnotes in italics to clarify something or add additional information or internet links. While some additions might seem pedantic, among the readers will be the great-grandchildren of Aubrey, to whom Fortnite is an on-line gaming craze (at least in 2019) and not the British term for a two-week period to which Aubrey was referring.

Country and city names are as they were at the time of the story, so in 1971 when Aubrey and Hulda go back for their fourth term, the country had just changed its name to Zaire. Thus, it stays that way until the end of the memoir, as it was four years after Aubrey passed away that the country reverted to its former name, DR Congo. The colonial city names changed in 1965: the pertinent ones in the story being Leopoldville to Kinshasa, Stanleyville to Kisangani, and Paulis to Isiro.

Ron encouraged Dad to begin the project many years ago. He wrote the Foreword and put together some of the pages that appeared as appendices in the blog version posted online in 2017 – www.aubreysbistro.wordpress.com .

Ron's, Ken's and my hope (and I'm sure Carol's hope as well, if she was still with us) is that Dad's story comes alive to the reader and that his journey from the past offers a fresh reminder of God's faithfulness in the present.

Dave Brown
Calgary, April 2019

Many audio and visual details such as maps, photographs, audio recordings and a family tree can be found in the blog version of this book.

aubreysbistro.wordpress.com

Chapter 1

Early Life
1911 to 1935

PAUL AND MARY BROWN ON THE OCCASION OF THEIR 50TH WED-
DING ANNIVERSARY, WITH THEIR FAMILY IN SUMMERFIELD, 1908

Beginnings

I, Aubrey Lewis Brown, was born in Eaglehawk, a little town four miles north of Bendigo in central Victoria, Australia on September 21, 1911.

My father, William Henry Brown, and my mother, Beatrice Janet Brown (nee Hocking) lived on a farm, twenty miles north of Bendigo at a place called Neilborough East.

My sister, Gladys Mary Brown, was born before me in the year 1910 on May 3rd, and my younger brother, Rupert William Brown, came into the world on March 19, 1916. His birth completed our happy family.

My grandparents on the Brown side were Paul and Mary Brown. They originally came from England and first settled on a farm northwest of Melbourne. Later they moved further north and settled on a farm in Summerfield, which was only four miles from where we lived. There were ten children in this Paul Brown family - five sons and five daughters.

When I was three or four years of age, I can remember Grandpa Brown coming to our house in a horse-drawn cart bringing us vegetables from his garden and grapes from the vines he had planted around his vegetable patch. I never knew Grandma Brown; she passed away before I was born.

The Paul Brown family was fond of singing and on a Sunday afternoon they would gather around an old pump organ. I can remember some of the uncles and aunties would sing for an hour or so from the Methodist Hymn Book. What harmony, all four parts! As I got older I joined in singing with them.

Edith was the youngest girl of this family and was the organist at Summerfield Methodist Church. In this church the old men would sit up in the front seats. I remember Grandpa Brown with his white beard sitting there in church with the other old men. When it came time to sing, his deep bass voice could easily be heard.

My mother's side was the Hocking family. Thomas Hocking came to Australia from Cornwall, England and passed away in 1896 before I was born. He married Margaret Morris, who was born in Merthyr Tydvil in Wales. She migrated to Australia with her parents at the age of seven and at the age of 18 she married Thomas Hocking. They had twelve children - seven daughters and five sons.

My mother Beatrice, and her twin sister Blanche, were born July 24th, 1881. Blanche died of typhoid fever at the age of 22.

The five Hocking boys were hard-working farmers and the youngest boy, Vernon, served in France in the First World War. I can remember the big welcome home party at the Hocking home when he returned after the end of the war in 1918.

According to service records at the National Archives of Australia, a private Vernon Arnold Hocking arrived home from service March 31, 1919 having served with the 5th Machine Gun Battalion. Service #508.

Preschool Years

Sunday was a special day each week. My father would hitch a horse to the double-seated buggy and drive us to church. He and Mom would sit in the front seat and we three children in the back seat. We would leave at 10:30 am every Sunday morning and it took us nearly half an hour to drive to the Summerfield Methodist Church* where we would all sit together as a family in church. I remember Mom would carry biscuits in her purse for the restless ones.

The Methodist Church joined with the Presbyterian and Congregational Churches to form the Uniting Church of Australia in 1977.

After church was over, Mom would take the three of us children to the Hocking home which was close by the church. Dad, however, would drive a mile or so on to the Brown home where he was raised and have Sunday dinner there. At 3 pm, Mom's sister Ida, would take us to Sunday School for an hour. I remember the first time they tried to take me to Sunday School, I was so scared that I went halfway and then refused to go any further. The next Sunday I made it all the way. After Sunday School was over, Dad would pick us up and we would return home in time for my parents to do the chores.

Every year there would be a Sunday School Anniversary when there would be a special speaker and musical numbers by the children. I will never forget the first anniversary I attended. Mom had bought me a new little suit and a new hat. I marched with the other children to the platform and when we were seated I could not find a place to hang my new hat, so I sat on it! The poor hat was knocked out of shape and after the service I was asked, "Why did you do such a thing?"

During my preschool years I would go with Mom to milk the cows, feed the calves and chickens and then in the evening I would help her gather the eggs. Dad was away most of the day working on the fields. During harvest time, we children would already be in bed before he would return home with his team of horses.

Every Thursday, the grocer would call for our produce and bring groceries that Mom had ordered the week before. Driving a pair of horses hitched to a covered wagon, he came from a town six miles away and would visit all the farm houses. Sometimes Mom would have a cream can full of cream which he would take to market to sell, and sometimes a box with several pounds of butter which Dad and Mom would have churned at night after we children were in bed. Then there would be a box with several dozen eggs to give to the grocer to sell. Lastly, he would take Mom's new list of groceries and then buy and bring them to us the following Thursday.

Every Tuesday and Saturday the baker would come to our house in his delivery cart with fresh bread. Sometimes, though, Mom would make bread and buns.

An interesting day for us children was when Mom and Dad would take us shopping in Bendigo, the closest city to our farm. As this was before there were any cars around, we did the three-hour trip by horse and buggy. We had to get up extra early to do the morning chores and then we would leave around 8 am, taking sandwiches to eat along the way. We would arrive in the city around 11 am and leave the horse and buggy at the livery stables. This was like a parking lot, where between forty and sixty horses were tied up in stalls, fed and watered. Troughs of water were also supplied along the road where horses could drink.

Parked in the centre part of the stable were all the different kinds of buggies and wagons the farmers used, all neatly arranged in rows. When it came time to return home around 3 pm, the stable attendant would find our horse, untie it and hitch it to our buggy. After Dad had paid the stable attendant, we would start the three-hour, twenty-mile journey home.

Sometimes on these trips to Bendigo, we would take things to sell, like a dozen young roosters or old hens, sheep or rabbit skins. Then on our return we would bring home cases of tomatoes, apples and other kinds of fruit which we didn't grow in our own orchard.

These trips to the city happened about three times a year for us children and one of the highlights for us children was to have a meal in a restaurant. Generally, it was a pasty (*meat and vegetable pie*) with hot chocolate.

RUPERT, AUBREY AND GLADYS, 1920

WILLIAM AND BEATRICE BROWN WITH THEIR CHILDREN AUBREY, GLADYS AND RUPERT (L-R) IN BENDIGO, 1929

School Days

When I reached the age of six, I started school in the village of Neilborough East. Schools in the farming districts were generally a one-room school - one teacher for twenty to thirty children in grades one to eight.

At Neilborough East Elementary School, I learned to read, write, and do arithmetic. In Grade 3, the teacher put me into Grade 4 for the second half of that year. Our school started the first week in February and went right through until a few days before Christmas. We had a one-week holiday at Easter and another week holiday in September.

I remember a minister would come at times to give us religious instruction from the Bible and teach us songs. One song I remember was "I am so glad that our Father in Heaven tells of His love in the Book He has given."

My sister and I used to walk the one and a half miles to school. We tried to leave home at 8:30 am with the lunches Mom made for us, and would return home by 4 pm. When we were older, we had to help with the chores before we went to school, which meant that after breakfast both my sister and I would milk two or three cows each, and then get ready for school. Mom would finish the milking because by then Dad was already working in the fields.

After school, I would ride a pony to fetch the eight cows and then start the milking process all over again. The milk had to be put through a separator and the skim milk was fed to the calves, dogs, cats, and pigs.

When I finished grade eight, I passed an exam and was awarded a Certificate of Merit which I still have.

Only a few privileged children were able to continue their education past Grade 8. The larger towns and cities were the only places that had high schools and there were no cars or buses in those days to take teenagers to school. So, unless a person had a relative in town or a friend where one could board, high school was usually out of the question.

For our family, there was no way for to keep attending school.

NEILBOROUGH EAST SCHOOL, 1920

Farming

At the age of thirteen and shortly after completing Grade 8, I left school. My father needed help on the expanding farm because he had just purchased another two hundred acres of wooded land adjoining his farm. In our spare time we had to remove the trees and stumps and clear the land for cultivation.

At this time my father taught me to drive a team of three horses. It was seeding time, so as Dad was seeding with his team of horses, I came behind with my team and the harrow. We would walk up and down the field all day long.

Seeding was done in Australia during April and May, then in June and July farmers would plough the paddocks (*fields*) that were to be seeded the following year. This was called fallow and Dad would drive a six-horse team pulling a four-furrow plough. I would follow behind him driving a three-horse team pulling a double-furrow plough.

There were no tractors in those days, so farming was much slower than it is today with the help of modern equipment.* We were up at 5 am to feed the horses, an hour before our own breakfast. At 6:30 we would go to the stable to groom the horses with a curry-comb and brush. Then we would harness them for work, first putting on the huge collar, then the winkers which went on the head holding the bit in their mouths so they could be guided. By 7 am we would have yoked the horses to the plough and be ready to start the day's work just as it was starting to get light. We would bring the horses back at noon for a drink and another feed of chaff mixed with grain. After about an hour we would return them to the plough and work until we couldn't see anymore. This was our winter; there were fewer daylight hours in which to work. When we returned home we fed the horses again for two hours before turning them loose on the grass overnight.

* A few tractors were making their appearance in the 1920s, but it wasn't until after WWII when farmers had made it through the economically depressed 1930s and then the second World War, that tractors finally replaced most horses on the farms.

As I got older, I was given a six-horse team to drive and eventually it was an eight-horse team for which I was responsible. In this team, there were four leaders and four followers in tandem. By the time my younger brother finished school, we had two eight-horse teams working and a few spare horses to take the place of any that got sick.

I found out in farming that man can sow the seed, but only God could give the increase or the harvest. We had good seasons and bad seasons. Some years the price of wheat was good, other years the price went down, but every year we sowed in hope.

In the district where I was raised, most of the farmers did mixed farming. That meant we didn't have to rely on just one crop for existence. Most farmers raised sheep and on our farm, we had three to four hundred sheep. Each year we would have a crop of lambs to sell and also a crop of wool. At an early age I learned to tend the sheep, especially during the lambing season.

Dad also taught me to shear sheep. At first, we sheared off the wool with blades which were like a big pair of scissors. Later on, shearing machines were invented and they were like a hair clipper that barbers use to cut hair, only a bit wider. This helped us to shear quicker and easier. Shearing was a hot, back-aching job and while most experienced shearers could shear a hundred sheep in one day, the majority of us could only do seventy to eighty sheep.

After the sheep had been shorn, we had to know how to pick up the fleece and spread it out on a table. After taking away any soiled wool, along with burrs and thistles, we would fold it up and put it into a bale and press it down. When a bale was full it was sewn up, stenciled and ready to go off to market. The newly-shorn sheep would be branded *WB* with a tar-like branding oil, so one could find them if they strayed into the neighbour's flock.

With a good-sized flock of sheep on the farm, we could select young sheep for butchering. Dad showed me how to butcher, something we always did towards evening time. After removing the skin from the sheep, we would hang the carcass up overnight for the meat to set. On the next morning, we cut the meat up into various sizes and put it into sacks to be stored in a cool place as there were no freezers or refrigerators in those days.

We enjoyed plenty of fresh meat on the farm. Our favourite meal was roast mutton, roast potatoes, mint sauce, vegetables from the garden and sometimes Yorkshire pudding.

The fat removed from the carcass would be boiled and poured into a pail. When it became cold and set, it was called dripping. We used this for frying, and I remember when hard times came and money was scarce, we couldn't afford to use butter or margarine, so we spread dripping on our bread.

We were never without work on the farm. After the seed was planted, and the land plowed up for the following year, then the fallow had to be cultivated. When field work with the horse teams finished, we would work on clearing new land. Trees had to be burnt down, cut up and removed. Rocks had to be dug out and all the bush cleared away ready for the plough.

In October, we would start shearing sheep because by then the cold weather was already over. By November we would start cutting hay. We cut both oat and wheat crops to feed our horses and sometimes even the cattle when it was a dry season.

The crops were cut by a reaper and binder which produced the sheaves, and these had to be stooked (*stood up against each other*) so that the sheaves could dry before they were built into a stack of hay. We tried to get all the hay in by the end of November.

December was harvest month with its long days and hot weather. The wheat was put into sacks and carted to the nearest railway station where it was sold. Some sacks of wheat were kept back for seed for the following year and some used for chicken feed. These sacks would hold three bushels and each weighed one hundred and eighty pounds. We had to carry these sacks on our backs from the wagon to the barn. The sacks of oats were much lighter, weighing one hundred and twenty pounds each or forty pounds to a bushel.

When the harvest was all in, we would cut some of the straw and use it to thatch our hay stacks. These stacks were out in the open and the thatch would allow the water to run off so the hay would not get wet and thus rot. A man who owned a steam engine and a chaff cutter would visit the farms and cut the hay into chaff. In later years, we bought our own outfit and didn't have to depend on outside help.

WILLIAM, AUBREY AND RUPERT WITH THE HORSES, CIRCA 1930

Conversion

The most important thing in my life took place when I was fourteen years of age. It was on April 25th, 1926 that I became a Christian. I was not a Christian because I was raised in a Christian home, nor was I a Christian because I regularly attended church and Sunday School or because I lived in a so-called Christian country.

It was in Sunday School on this special Sunday afternoon when, instead of classes, we had an open session with a visiting speaker. His name was Rev. George Beckett, a Methodist evangelist who had come to hold ten days of meetings. He showed us plainly from the Scriptures that all had sinned, all were guilty before God, and that all needed to repent and accept what a loving God provided for guilty sinners. God's only Son, the Lord Jesus Christ, had died on the cross to pay the penalty for our sins. That remedy provided for lost sinners, could either be accepted or rejected. An altar call was made, and I was one of the first to raise my hand showing that I understood and was ready to receive Christ into my heart. Oh, the joy and peace of receiving forgiveness of sins at the foot of the cross. That day, my name was crossed off the list in the book of those waiting for judgment and was written into the Lamb's Book of Life. Those ten days of meetings were well attended and blessed by God and our church was revived.

To help the new converts grow in their new faith, a Christian Endeavor Society was formed in the local church. These CE meetings were held every Wednesday evening for the teenagers and others who wanted to come. During these meetings every believer was asked to take part; some were chosen to write an essay on a Bible character or a Bible subject. One would be chosen to select songs and help lead the meeting with an adult. Once a month, a consecration meeting would be held when the local minister would come and bring a message. At the close, all would stand and repeat the CE pledge. This is the pledge put to song:

Now trusting in the Lord for strength,
this promise I can make
That I should try to do His will, to live for Jesus' sake.
My rule of life shall be to pray, my Bible daily read
To help my church in every way, her services to heed.
Throughout the week when ere she called or
on the Sabbath Day
I shall be there unless He leads my steps another way.
Endeavor meetings i'll attend, when ere that meeting be
To all my duties i'll be true, no silence there for me.
If hindered by the Lord my God, i'll not forgetful be
But send a consecration verse, which may be read for me.

There were also sentence prayers at these meetings, when new Christians were encouraged to pray in public. During prayer time we would all kneel down. The well-known consecration hymn was sung at these monthly meetings: *Take My Life and Let It Be.*

Teen Years

My teenage years were never dull. I enjoyed the outdoor life in the warm sunshine with plenty of hard work, good food, social activities, and gathering with relatives and friends at church every Sunday.

A cricket team was formed at Summerfield and I joined up and learned to play as part of a team, even though as a boy at school I had already learned how to play cricket. We had one mid-week practice and on Saturday afternoons we would play against neighboring teams. I played for several years and one year I was awarded a new cricket bat for the best batting average on the team. Cricket is a good clean sport. There are eleven men on a cricket team and it is played mostly in England, Australia, India, Pakistan, and the West Indies. There were no organized sports played on Sundays back in the 1920s and 1930s.

To raise money for our local cricket club we would arrange a hare shoot. After meeting at a certain farm where we knew hares were plentiful, we would divide the twenty-five to thirty of us into four groups and each group would take a side, some on the north, others the east, and others on the south and west sides. A shot was fired by the captain and we would all start walking towards the center of the field. The hares would be aroused and would run to escape but were shot on the run. When we arrived in the center the 20 to 30 hares were skinned and then we would decide on the next area to encircle. We did that all day long. The hare skins were dried and sold, and with the money we earned, we bought cricket equipment.

On most of the farms there was no lack of ponies and light horses to ride. This was great fun and some children would ride to school on ponies. One of our favourite chores after school was to catch a horse, put on the bridle and saddle and ride the four miles to pick up the mail at the Summerfield Post Office. We would also pick up the daily newspaper from the city, The Bendigo Advertiser *(which is still Bendigo's newspaper)*, which gave us not only the local news but also what was happening in overseas countries. The paper was important for us as there were no radio or television sets in those days.

THE SUMMERFIELD CRICKET TEAM, 1933

The Call

1935

The leaders of the Summerfield Methodist Church where I attended planned a series of meetings with a young preacher from England as the special speaker. Her name was Sister Ida. She was in her early twenties when she visited Australia and had been preaching for a number of years. I was nineteen years old at this time and I never missed one meeting during the ten days. This lady preached with power and a special anointing of the Holy Spirit was upon her. It was during these meetings that I made a full surrender of my life to God.

I was now willing to do anything and go anywhere for my Saviour and Lord. God, by His Spirit had done a needed work in my heart and it seemed that our whole church was revived.

A dear saint of God in our church saw the need to commence a class for the young men attending the Sunday morning worship service. This was a kind of a Bible class ending up with a prayer meeting and time of sharing.

A little while later the pastor began a theology class for any who were interested to begin preaching and seven of us joined up. Not long after that, church services would be arranged for the budding preachers and two or three of us would take part as a team. The end result of that class was that all of us seven passed our theology exams and our trial sermons, one written and one preached. We became accredited local preachers of the Methodist Church and were scheduled for two or three preaching appointments a month for a start. From then on, I preached for fifty years.

During this time, the pastor of the Raywood Circuit approached me one day and asked me if I would be interested in opening up a Sunday School in the village of Neilborough where I had gone to elementary school. This was a distance of six miles from where we lived. After praying about the matter I felt I should go. It would give the children in that area a chance to hear the gospel. We visited homes and advertised when the Sunday School would be opened. The pastor came and held an induction service and the following Sunday we started. Thirty girls and boys showed up for the start and they continued to come Sunday by Sunday, even though some were from godless homes.

A series of evangelistic meetings were held in that district later on. The prayer meetings were held a little distance away in a dance hall and some nights we were pelted with rocks. What a noise as the rocks hit the corrugated iron roof. Satan didn't like us praying there, but some souls came to the Lord during these years.

After waiting on the Lord for guidance as to what my life's work should be, the answer came in June of 1935, just before my 24th birthday.

A friend of mine, Harold Williams, was returning from the Belgian Congo in Africa, and he was scheduled to hold a meeting in the Yalook Church about fifteen miles from home. I attended this meeting and saw slides of his missionary work in the Congo. I took home with me some free literature and the following day when I was alone in my room reading these leaflets, a passage of scripture in bold print stood out. It was from Isaiah 6:8: *"Then I heard the voice of the Lord saying, Whom shall I send, and who will go for us?"* I knew this was God's voice speaking to me and I responded there and then, "Lord, here am I. Send me." Now the battle was on and the devil tried to discourage and stop me.

By September, I was enrolled in a two-year program of studies at Melbourne Bible Institute.

Chapter 2

Training
1935 to 1939

Aubrey's graduating class from Melbourne Bible Institute, 1938

Melbourne Bible Institute

September 1935 to August 1937

In September of 1935, I started my studies at Melbourne Bible Institute. Here I studied the Bible for two years with each year divided into three trimesters and would be equivalent to three years of study at a Canadian Bible school. What blessed years they were! I stayed at the Men's Training Home next door to MBI.

MBI, now known as Melbourne School of Theology is still going strong today.

At the start there were a lot of rules and regulations to get used to at the school. Rising time was at 6 am with half an hour to shower, shave and get ready for an hour's Quiet Time. After that we had to make our bed, clean the room and be ready for breakfast at 8 am. I must say here that the one-hour Quiet Time became very precious to me, a time of reading the Bible and then a time of worship, praise and prayer. From Bible School days and onward I have always tried to maintain that early morning hour with the Lord; that seemed to make the day right. Some days, when traveling, it wasn't always convenient to have devotions in the morning and it had to work in to another part of the day. This habit was something I learned at MBI and followed all these years since with no regrets. One cannot live the Christian life without it.

The first week, I was sent out with the rest of the men to give Religious Instruction in a city school. After I got used to riding my bicycle through city traffic, I enjoyed the 9 am Religious Instruction classes every Wednesday. On Friday mornings after the missionary meeting, prayer was offered and while still kneeling, we would all repeat the refrain from Joshua 1:16, *"All that Thou commandest us we will do, and whithersoever Thou sendest us, we will go."*

Every week we had to attend two open-air street meetings, one on Friday night in a shopping area, and another on Sunday night in another suburb. In my second year, I became leader of an Open Air* group and was responsible for the meeting.

Open Air Campaigners are still active today in Australia and worldwide.

My last two terms at MBI, I was chosen to be one of the three Senior Men Students. We had special responsibilities placed upon us and I learned a lot. This was good training for future service.

During the two years I spent in Melbourne I had an opportunity to attend the monthly prayer meeting of a mission group called Worldwide Evangelization Crusade (WEC). It was held on a Saturday afternoon at the Keswick Book Room. There I got to know several of the Melbourne Council members of WEC and others who came to pray. When my two years of Bible study were nearing completion, I applied to WEC and was accepted. As they had no headquarters in Australia in 1937, the Council asked me to go to the main WEC headquarters in London, England for orientation and further training.

In August of 1937, I graduated and received my Bible School Diploma.

I then returned home and took my younger brother Rupert's place on the farm so he could have the chance to study the Bible at the same school. He was able to finish two terms before it was time for me to leave for England.

I said goodbye to my parents on the farm and went to Melbourne where I stayed at MBI to take care of final departure details.

THE STRATHEDEN PASSENGER LINER IN MELBOURNE HARBOUR, 1938

From Melbourne to London

February 22, 1938 to April 1, 1938

I set sail on the 23,500-ton ocean liner called the Stratheden, and six weeks later docked in London, England on the 1st of April. I was twenty-six years of age.

At the Melbourne docks on February 22, I said good-bye to my sister and brother, a few other relative and friends, as well as some MBI students who had come down to see me off. It was a great farewell and at that time I didn't know that thirteen years would pass before I would see Australia again.

Passengers on departing ships at that time had a tradition of throwing rolls of paper streamers to their loved ones on shore, who would hold them until they broke as the ship sailed away. With my last streamer broken and as I was losing sight of my loved ones, I returned to my cabin and found a welcome surprise. On my bed were many farewell letters, cards and gifts of fruit which helped ease the increasing sense of loneliness that I was beginning to feel. I didn't know any person on board and I had the four-bunk cabin to myself from Melbourne to Adelaide. Everything was so new to me because I hadn't been on an ocean liner before, but I soon found new friends.

The following incidents are taken from letters which I had written home to my parents and are in diary form:

February 22, Left Melbourne

February 27, Left Fremantle
Perth's port city.
We had a good voyage across the Australian Bight between Adelaide and Perth on the West coast. These are the dates when we are due to arrive in ports along the way:

March 8—Colombo, Ceylon
March 12—Bombay, India
March 16—Aden, Yemen
March 20—Port Said, Egypt
March 23—Malta
March 25—Marseilles, France
March 28—Gibraltar
March 28—Tangier, Morocco
March 31—Plymouth, England
April 1—Tilbury Docks, London, England

March 5
We travel about 400 miles a day and although we are nearing the equator, the weather is not too hot. Since last writing, I have met some Christian people and we arranged to meet on deck at 8 am for a time of prayer and Bible study. We are going to hold a children's meeting next Sunday.

Yesterday, about halfway between Freemantle and Columbo, we passed what are called the Cocos or Keeling Islands. There are only a few people who live there and we dropped a barrel of something for them. They came out in a sailing boat to pick it up.

Captain Harrison led Divine Service on Sunday morning (*Lutheran liturgical service*). The steward gave us permission to hold our little meeting in the nursery last night and ten of us had Bible reading, prayer and fellowship.

Flying fish can be seen at times. They rise up out of the water and fly just like a bird for a hundred yards and then disappear into the water.

March 10 – Colombo
Colombo is the port city and capital of Ceylon, now called Sri Lanka since 1972.

After going ashore at Colombo, I first went to the Post Office, bought some stamps and posted letters. Then I took a rickshaw to a nearby park and gardens where for the first time I saw cinnamon plants, rubber, coffee and mango trees, and the plants that produce vanilla beans and cocoa pods from which chocolate is made. Then I visited a Buddhist temple where I saw my first scene of idolatry. A man was kneeling with his face nearly to the floor, praying to his god which was a piece of wood - an image of Buddha.

Later that day I was resting in a church. A man came in with such a beautiful face. After we talked for a while, he told me he was a converted Buddhist and had been preaching the Gospel for forty years. For the first time, I knelt with a dark-skinned man and together we had prayer. He suggested it and he prayed, then he asked me to pray. He preaches in prisons, churches and in the open air (*public spaces*).

At one shop I went into, I bought a red lead pencil and gave the shop keeper a gospel of John. His face lit up and asked, "Are you a Christian too? We are also Christians in this shop."

After Colombo, our next stop will be Bombay, 890 miles away.

March 15 - Bombay
India's largest city, called Mumbai since 1995.

We will arrive in Aden tomorrow. I went ashore in Bombay for two hours and stopped to watch the Indians doing construction work. Both men and women were working on the building. The women were carrying the concrete in bowls on their heads and at a certain place they would then pass it from one to another until the concrete reached to the top of the building.

A number of people got on board at Bombay making our total number of passengers now 1063.

The purser gave us permission to have our daily devotional meeting in the dining saloon at 11 am and yesterday morning, seventeen people came. I led the meeting and gave my testimony. This morning, another missionary led the meeting.

It is 1600 miles from Bombay to London.

March 18 - Aden
Aden is the port city of Yemen, at the bottom of the Arabian Peninsula and at the eastern entrance to the Red Sea.

The Stratheden docked at Aden on Wednesday. It hadn't rained for two years and there wasn't much vegetation to be see. I went ashore with five other young men and we went sightseeing in a Ford V8 for which we each had to pay the driver five shillings. The main industries we saw were salt and fish. The salt works were interesting with their huge windmills that pumped water from the sea into huge pans (*basins*) of various sizes, some as large as one acre. After the sun had dried up the water, workmen would go and scrape up the salt and put it into railway boxcars which were pulled by camels to large heaps where the salt was emptied out.

We visited the ancient water tanks (*called the Cisterns of Tawila*) which are believed to have been made about 650 BC. They were found by the British in 1854 all covered over with sand and rubbish and when cleaned out, they would hold twenty million gallons of water. There were seven tanks and all were dry.

As Aden was a duty-free port, things were cheaper to buy there than at other places.

There are now twenty people who regularly attend our daily Bible studies led by a Baptist teacher named Dr. Neighbor.

March 21 - Suez
Suez is an Egyptian city at the southern end of the Suez Canal, where the Red Sea narrows into the Gulf of Suez.

At 6 am on Sunday morning, we arrived at Suez where we stopped for one hour before entering the Suez Canal. Thirty or so passengers went ashore and made the trip to Cairo by cars and then met up with us again at Port Said. It was very interesting to see at close range, the ships coming out of the canal and the others waiting to go through as only in certain parts is the canal wide enough for ships to pass each other. When it was our turn, five ships went ahead of us and one followed.

Suez is a very ancient city. We could only see it in the distance about half a mile away from the southern entrance of the canal. It was a place of importance when the overland route to India was opened up in 1842. The P&O Company (*which owned the Stratheden*) at one time had 3000 camels employed in taking passengers, mail and stores (*supplies*) across from Cairo to Suez and back. Later came the railway and later still the canal was made.

Fourteen miles from the canal's southern entrance lay the Bitter Lakes extending for about eighteen miles and it is here that the ships can pass each other. A few miles further north is Lake Timsah, and seventeen miles further is Kantara, where the railway station marks the terminus of the rail line to Palestine. Port Said lies about twenty-four miles due north of Kantara.

In 1856 the Suez Canal Company was formed. The canal took ten years to construct and cost £29,725,000 to construct. It was formally opened in 1869 and is 87.5 miles long. It is about 118 feet wide and thirty-three feet deep. Vessels of thirty feet draught are allowed to pass through.

The speed of large vessels in the canal is limited to five-and-a-half miles per hour; otherwise the waves created would destroy the sides of the canal. It takes twelve hours to pass through the canal. The ships would speed up when they come to a lake in the middle of the canal (*Great Bitter Lake*).

Canal dues on a vessel of approximately 16,000 tons amount to about £3000 for each passage. About ten vessels a day pass through the canal on average. A large portion of the money goes towards maintaining the canal and increasing its width and depth. There is an asphalt road alongside the canal as well as a railway line. Two of our passengers rode their bikes from Suez to Port Said (*while the ship made its way slowly through the canal*).

At one place there was a jolt as we struck bottom and at another place the ship got too near the side going around a bend and got stuck for five hours. We learned later that one propeller was damaged because of the mud. We finally arrived at Port Said at one o'clock in the morning, five hours late. At that early hour I went ashore with others to visit a big department store. We left Port Said at 7 am and not far out on one of the break waters is a huge monument of Lesseps to whose genius the canal is due. This was our first view of the Mediterranean Sea with its deep blue water.

One day, a notice was put up for any passengers who would like to visit the engine room. They could do so between ten and eleven o'clock. This was too good to miss, so I went. The ship was driven by thick oil like tar which is heated to a temperature of 200 degrees before being sprayed into the cylinders and fired. They used about 90 tons of oil a day averaging 20 miles per hour or 16 knots.

Malta
Officially the Republic of Malta, a Southern European island country in the Mediterranean Sea.
We had a stopover of three hours at Malta and nearly all on board went ashore that afternoon. The streets are very narrow and steep and some bear the name of St. Paul. We read in the Bible, in the book of Acts, that Paul was there on his voyage to Rome.

We saw a man delivering fresh milk - extra fresh! He was driving a herd of goats up a side street. He would knock on a door and if the person wanted milk, he would milk a goat at the front door and sell it, then move on to the next customer. The customer had to hold the goat during the roiling process.

We visited a museum and shops selling lace and silk. The Maltese do beautiful work.

March 26 - Marseilles
Marseilles is France's port city and lies on the northern Mediterranean Sea.
Upon arrival yesterday morning at Marseilles, the Strathallan was there on her maiden voyage to Australia. This was the sister ship to our Stratheden and I suppose my last letter would go home on that boat.

Marseilles is the second largest city of France, and a busy port. We stayed there twenty-four hours. On returning from a walk in the city along the docks, I counted fifty different ships loading and unloading.

Two men died on board the day before we reached Marseilles. One was an elderly gentleman who used to sit across from me at meal times. He was found dead in bed from a heart attack. The other man fell down the steps in the engine room and broke his neck. After leaving Marseilles and two hours out to sea, the ship slowed up and these two bodies were buried in the watery deep.

Sunday, March 27
I have just returned from Sunday School where I was asked to take charge today as the other man was sick. Twelve little boys and girls met together in the nursery and some mothers came as well. We had a good time. Talking with one of the mothers afterwards, she told me that it was the first time her girl had been to Sunday School. She said that she was on her way to Scotland from the jungles of India and that where they lived, they only had church services every three months.

There is one more event that took place on this voyage. One day a man approached me and asked if I was a Christian. I replied that yes, I was a Christian. His second question was: "Are you a baptized believer? When I told him that I had not yet been baptized, he replied, "Here is water, what is hindering you from being baptized?" He said he was willing to go with me to the bathroom and baptize me in a tub of water. I told him that I wasn't ready yet and that I would think it over. Meeting this man was a challenge to me and made me think. I received baptism later in England.

We had a short stopover at Gibraltar where I went ashore. After leaving there we sailed through the Strait of Gibraltar a few miles to Tangier for a short stay. Then it was on to our last stop at Plymouth on the south coast of England, before heading to our final destination - Tilbury Docks. We arrived safely in London on April 1.

A great look at the history of the Stratheden, with images of the streamer tradition and some interior photos is shown on this web site: www.pandosnco.co.uk/stratheden.html

Portrait of Aubrey, circa 1938

Missionary Training in England

April 1938 to April 1939

April 1, I arrived at Tilbury Docks and passed through customs, took a train to the heart of London, and then a taxi to the headquarters of Worldwide Evangelization Crusade. For the following months I lived in the Crystal Palace area of south London and my address was: 19 Highland Rd. Upper Norwood SE 19, London.

The WEC HQ consisted of three main buildings: #17 Highland Road, the original home of Mr. and Mrs. C.T. Studd; #19 Highland Road next door, the new three-story hostel nearing completion; and across the street was #34, the home of a friend of WEC who took in several candidates and fed them free of charge as her service to the Lord.

Behind #19 was an old coach house with stables and a hay loft. This building had been renovated and the hay loft was now being used as a men's dormitory. Other rooms were used as mission offices, storage for missionary equipment, and a place where missionaries packed their outfits for the fields.

It was great on arriving at HQ to meet my old friend Elijah Bingham. We were students together at MBI in Melbourne and we roomed together in the hay loft with six other male candidates until the new hostel was ready for occupancy. When it opened, we took over the third story of the hostel and had some wonderful time of prayer and fellowship.

The daily schedule at HQ went something like this: rise at 6 am and wash, shave, make our beds and then Quiet Time until 7:30. Then we did chores until 8:15 when we had breakfast. For breakfast we had porridge, fried potatoes and sometimes bacon. We used tin plates and cups (some of the cups had no handles); we had no table cloth, but we usually had plenty to eat and drink. Our main meal was dinner at 1 pm followed by tea time at 4:30 and supper at 7:30 pm. For supper we had bread and dripping, jam and cocoa. When the loaf of bread was gone the meal was finished.

At 9 am staff and candidates met each day for a meeting. Candidates received instruction by way of a message given on several topics relating to faith and missionary work. Letters were read from the fields. Then we knelt down and had a session of worship, praise, and intercession. This meeting generally went on for two hours, sometimes until 11:30 am. What blessed times they were! Then we would go to our different assignments: some working on the building projects, some doing laundry, some doing language study.

The first night at HQ, I had a lesson in French. A candidate who had just returned from France was our teacher, and there were three of us heading for the Belgian Congo who were in this class.

The candidate secretary was Mr. Sutton. We each had to hand in to him £35 (*which was then around CDN $110*) for purchasing our outfit for the field. They purchased it and packed it for us; very simple in those days. Life at HQ became very interesting for me. It was a busy place with candidates and missionaries continually coming and going; some to and from the fields and others to language studies in Belgium, France or Portugal. When there was time off, I would visit the historic places in London such as Buckingham Palace, Westminster Abbey, Trafalgar Square, Tower of London, Science Museum, Hyde Park, Dr. Campbell Morgan's church, Wesley Chapel, John Wesley's grave, the Parliament Buildings with Big Ben, and the London Zoo.

In May, I had the privilege of conducting a service in England. It was in a Mission Hall in Bermondsey, out in a slum area of east-end London and the people looked very poor. I had a children's meeting at 7 pm and the evening service at

8:15. It took me an hour to get home travelling by tram and train. On Sunday afternoons I often went to an orphanage.

At HQ we heard news of the revival going on in Budapest. Some 8000 people attended meetings of James Stewart's evangelistic crusade in Eastern Europe. That was where Dr. Neighbor, the Bible teacher who taught our class on the ship, was heading.

One day I visited Croydon Airport not far from where I was staying.* Another day I saw about 60 airplanes flying together over London. It seemed to me that England was preparing for war; people were being taught how to make air raid precautions and how to wear gas masks.

* Croydon Airport was London's major airport in the 1930s. About fifteen months after Aubrey's visit, World War II started in September 1939 and the airport was closed to civilian flights. It was then converted to an air force base which played a major role in the Battle of Britain. Croydon was bombed heavily by the Germans in one of the first bombing raids in August 1940.

In June, owing to a shortage of women candidates*, the staff asked the men to help in the kitchen. One man who had some experience was chosen, and I was asked to be his helper and learn from him. After a month I had to be responsible to cook the meals for twenty-four people and train another candidate for the following month. This was just what I wanted before I left for Africa. The main cook, Mrs. Purves, would come each day into the kitchen and pray with us for money to buy groceries and make out the menu for the following day. Then we were left to make simple meals for our fellow candidates. We would start work at 7:30 am and keep going all day. We did the shopping every day from the shops that were close to the HQ. Food seemed cheap and we could get by on about ten shillings a day. Interested folks would give potatoes and other items to the Mission.

* It has only been in the last thirty years or so that men have felt comfortable in the kitchen. In the late 1930s, it was not looked on as proper for men to prepare meals, other than in a professional capacity, so most men would not have had any idea of how to cook.

After some months of prayer, consideration, and thought, I felt I should be baptized. The Lord's command was to go into all the world and preach the gospel and baptize those who believed. I was aware that this was being done by our Mission in the Congo. I contacted the local Baptist pastor and he invited me to attend his next baptismal classes which I did. Then after receiving instruction the pastor arranged for me, along with two others, to be baptized in the evening service on July 10th, 1938. This was a great experience in my life, as I obeyed the Lord's command and gave my testimony before going down under the water.

The candidates at HQ did a lot of open-air preaching in Upper Norwood. Sometimes the Salvation Army would join with us. I used to attend the Salvation Army meetings when I was free on Sundays as they had a good band and choir, and souls came to the Lord continually in their meetings.

One afternoon I was sent to take a mother's meeting in a Congregational Church; about 45 women turned up. They gave me a cup of tea before I started. When I was introduced, they all clapped, and when I finished speaking, they all clapped again. I didn't know whether it was for an encore or whether they were glad that I was finished! Some of the women looked as hard as nails and I doubt many of them would have gone to church.

Another time a party of eighteen young people from Ireland came to visit the headquarters for two days. The male candidates had to give up our beds for the visitors and we moved over to the Missionary Training Colony* not far away. We had to have two sittings for meals. I was on duty and for breakfast toasted three loaves of bread. We would buy a two-pound loaf of bread for four pence and use eight loaves of bread a day. The next week we started making jam. With some money that was sent in to the Mission we bought some Australian dried apricots to start with. The following week we had five sacks of rice, oatmeal, lentils, pea flour, and split peas sent to us. Sometimes we did not know where these items came from. It came in answer to prayer and God will reward the givers.

*Missionary Training Colony was a college founded by Capt. Godfrey Buxton, a decorated WWI veteran who had been wounded and was unable to walk without canes. He was thus unable to fulfill his desire to go to the mission field like his father Rev. Barclay Buxton, founder of the Japan Evangelistic Band. He decided to do what he could do and start a training centre for missionaries. He took over a vacant and unused college building in Upper Norwood, London in 1923.

I was asked to carry on with the cooking for the month of August, as several were going on holidays. However, I was relieved from the kitchen the last two weeks in August. This worked out well as my friend, Elijah Bingham, asked me to accompany him on a two-week bicycle tour to Wales and back. Elijah had relatives to visit and he wanted to visit the place where he was born.

One day the office secretary came down into the kitchen and asked if we would like to see something nice. She showed us a letter that contained a cheque for £1000. We had a good look at the cheque and handled it - something unusual for most of us. It was ear-marked for general funds and was something we had been praying for and expecting as there was a need for these funds. We never knew who sent it.

The second week in August we moved into the newly-finished hostel and I had the honor of cooking the first meal to be eaten there. I was also the last cook in the #17 home for staff and candidates. With my work of two and a half months finished in the kitchen, Mrs. Purves came and thanked me for my faithfulness in cooking during that time.

The summer holidays arrived and it was time for Elijah and I to focus on our trek. We had earlier written to friends of WEC to try and arrange meetings for us. Our plans were to visit the following cities: Reading, Wells, Western Super Mare, Cardiff, Swansea, Cheltenham, and Oxford.

We started out on our bicycles at 5:30 am from HQ and got out of London before the heavy traffic started. We stayed a while and were shown around Windsor Castle including the chapel where royalty worshipped. We had a good meeting that evening in Reading. The next day we rode on and during the day gave out many tracts and gospel portions. We rode on until it got dark and then camped for the night alongside a little hay stack. Next day we pushed on and it began to rain. We got soaking wet but kept going until we arrived at Wells. There we were welcomed and cared for. The two of us conducted an open-air meeting in Cheddar that evening and several Christians came and joined us as we preached the Gospel. Our next stop was Western Super Mare where we had a good response. Leaving there we crossed the Bristol Channel to Cardiff in Wales where we visited Elijah's relatives. I took a photo of a 400-year-old house with a thatch roof, before crossing into Wales. There were several old houses with thatch roofs.

We visited Swansea and went north to another place where we had a good meeting. The Welsh people really sang out and enjoyed it. In the home where we stayed, our host and hostess spoke to each other in Welsh, and we wondered what were they saying about their two visitors.

The next day we went sixteen miles further north to Aberdare. As no one offered us a meal or a bed, we bought some food and started an open-air meeting in the town square. Twelve or so Christians came and stood with us and we preached on until nearly eleven o'clock and then there was still a good crowd listening. We bought some more food and then slept under the stars down by the river. We left early next morning after taking a photo of the house where Elijah was born. Coming into Aberdare the evening previous, was the time the coal miners were coming home on bicycles from work, hundreds of them with black faces covered in coal dust. What a sight!

We then started our return journey to London, riding 70 miles to Cheltenham where we both preached in an Anglican Church. Church bells rang out at 7:30 pm and 70 people came to hear the two "Australian evangelists", at least this is what the Vicar called us when he introduced us to the congregation. One young fellow indicated he was willing to follow Christ.

Our next stop was Oxford, "city of spires".* We stayed there three days holding meetings every night. There was a response. We visited the university where 5000 students were studying. Our guide next took us to the place marked with a cross in the middle of a street in Oxford where Cranmer, Latimer, and Ridley were burnt at the stake.** We also saw the monuments of these three noble men who died for their faith and it brought a challenge to me to be ready.

* From a poem by Victorian poet Matthew Arnold, who called Oxford "the city of dreaming spires" after the stunning architecture of its university buildings.
** The Oxford Martyrs were Anglican bishops Hugh Latimer and Nicholas Ridley, and Archbishop Thomas Cranmer who were convicted of heresy in 1555, tied to a stake and burnt alive.

After one more stop in Reading we arrived safely back at HQ in London, tired but rejoicing. We had cycled 300 miles and taken 18 meetings in 18 days. What a delightful summer holiday! The countryside in England and Wales was really beautiful.

Life carried on as usual from September to the end of the year. One place I visited in London during this time was St. Paul's Cathedral. I also heard noted Australian evangelist, Rev. Lionel Fletcher, preach in a crusade at Croydon.

Letters were piling up that I could not answer and one day there came an offer from my uncle and auntie in Australia. Charles and Ida (*Hocking*) Wood offered to put out my prayer letter from time to time for my Australian relatives and friends. They faithfully did this for many years and I so much appreciated that. Keeping contact with one's friends is very important, especially those who pray for you.

In December, I received an invitation from some WEC friends in Reading to come and spend Christmas with them. I accepted the offer as I had a few days off and nowhere to go. This was my first Christmas away from home and these folks were so kind to me.

As Christmas day approached, boys and girls would come to the front door and sing Christmas carols, a wonderful custom here in England.

Just before I left HQ for the Christmas vacation, my close friend Ron Davis was leaving to go back to Kashmir. He had been there doing missionary work for three years and had to return to Britain for an operation. Ron was from Wales and had a deep love and passion for lost souls. He first went to Kashmir, when he was 21 years of age. During his second term, he was ambushed and killed by bandits.

As the new year of 1939 began, life at HQ continued to be a great learning experience. I heard new lessons in the life of faith and listened to experiences from missionaries who had spent several years on the field. New candidates were coming into HQ and others were having their farewells and going out to the mission field for the first time. I knew that my time was coming to go to France to study the French language, as I was next on the list. That day finally came, almost a year to the day from when I had first arrived in England. By the first of April, I joined six others in Paris who were already there studying French.

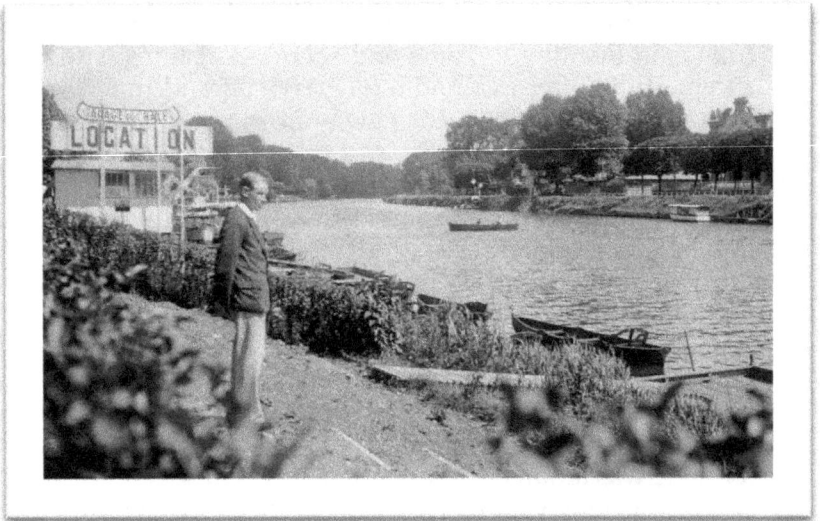

AUBREY AT THE MARNE RIVER IN FRANCE, CIRCA 1939

Language School in France

On April 1st of 1939, I was on my way to France. I left London by train going south to Newhaven where I caught the ferry across the English Channel to Dieppe. It took just over three hours to cross the channel. From Dieppe to St. Lazare station in Paris, I travelled by train. Arriving there, I was met by three of the WEC boys who took me to the underground railway which is called the metro here in France. These trains are fast and fairly cheap and we soon arrived at the Vincennes station where we caught a bus to the Bible Institute where I was booked in to stay. My address now changed to 39 Grande Rue, Nogent-sur-Marne, Seine, France.

The French Bible School was started in 1921 by Dr. and Mrs. Rueben Saillens. Their daughter, Mlle Saillens, was on staff there also. Dr. Saillens was then 84 years of age and was still active in teaching some subjects and on Sunday mornings he would preach sometimes for forty-five minutes in the chapel which was situated alongside the institute. This Bible School was small but was meeting a great need. There were fifteen students attending there when I arrived in April. I was with them for three months and attended the lectures to hear the French. At the end of June, they left for the summer vacation, but the WEC candidates and I stayed on during the summer.

My room was up on the third floor, sixty-five steps to climb every time I went from the dining room to my room. We were not allowed to speak English at meal time, so I was a pretty dumb person for the first few weeks!

43

As countries and peoples have different customs, so too, here in France I had to get used to sleeping on a square pillow. The French food was good, although some food we saw in the markets didn't tempt us, such as snails or frog legs which we didn't buy. Sometimes we ate dandelions as a vegetable. Passing by a butcher's shop one would see half of a horse in the window. Nothing else was sold in this shop apart from horse meat. At the school, a number of different kinds of cheese were on the table each day. Some I liked and others I didn't.

At Easter time, friends of WEC missionaries Jack Roberts and his sister Lily, came over from Wales to visit them. Jack and Lily were brushing up on their French before returning to Africa. During Easter holidays we were able to do some sightseeing all together. We went to Versailles on the west side of Paris to visit the palace of the former king of France, Louis XIV (1638-1715). We walked around inside the building for two hours and still didn't see everything. One room was three hundred feet long by sixty feet wide with lots of paintings on the walls. I saw a large table and was told that on this table on the eleventh day of the eleventh month of 1918, peace agreements were signed between the nations ending the First World War.*

* The Treaty of Versailles that was signed in the palace was actually done in June 28, 1919 after all the details were agreed upon, even though the war had officially ended as Aubrey says on November 11, 1918.

Another day we visited the Arc of Triumph, and then the Eiffel Tower which is 800 feet high. We visited Notre Dame, a Catholic cathedral in Paris, and on another day, we went to the palace at Fontainebleau that was used by Napoleon, thirty miles south of Paris.

During my stay in France, I was able to visit a Russian evangelical church in a community of 30,000 refugees. One lady, a Russian Baroness, had invited me to her home. She told me she had been in Australia and had visited Melbourne Bible Institute to speak there in 1926. She told me she was forced to leave Russia in 1923 for preaching the gospel. Amongst these Russian refugees a small Bible School had been started by Mr. Rees Howells of the Bible College of Wales, with twenty young Russian students attending.

Occasionally, I went out with the students and spent two or three hours at the market place with them. We set up a table and sold Christian literature, passed out tracts and did personal work. No preaching was allowed. We sang a few hymns and that surely gathered a crowd. One of the French boys told them we had Bibles and Testaments and other good books for sale. It was great to see some come forward and buy the New Testaments and Gospel portions.

In May I received some good mail from Australia. It was a letter from the Overseas Prayer Fellowship connected with the Free Tract Band. They told me that a dozen of their workers prayed for me regularly and this was a great encouragement. More prayer equals more power.

In July, I took a short course in French at the Alliance Francaise. I stayed at the Salvation Army in Paris during that time and really enjoyed those classes and found the study very profitable. At a Salvation Army meeting I gave my testimony in French for the first time. While in Paris, I also saw the prison cell where Madame Guyon was imprisoned.

July 14 is a great national holiday in France and my friends and I watched the long parade of soldiers and army vehicles which lasted three hours. The year of 1939 marked a special celebration to commemorate the 150th anniversary of the taking of the Bastille prison, the commencement of the French Revolution in 1789.

The flower gardens here in Paris look beautiful during the summer months. Although, as one walks along the streets, one can only see the tops of the houses. There are high walls around each house and the flowers and lawns are hidden from the public.

During August of 1939, the political situation was getting worse. It was announced over the radio that all British people should leave immediately. I went to the British Consul in Paris and had my passport registered. He advised me to leave France if I wasn't working. I didn't want to leave France as I knew I wouldn't get another opportunity to learn French before leaving for Congo. Dr. Saillens strongly urged me to stay, and as I prayed about the matter I felt I should stay a little longer. It was a risk. All the other candidates from WEC headquarters who were in France returned to London and I was now alone.

Everyone was expecting war. I listened to radio broadcasts from Britain at 10:30 am, 6 and 9 pm.

The feeling was tense in France and Dr. and Mrs. Saillens left for the country, as did the two girls in the kitchen who left for their home in the south of France. Only three of us were left at the Institute. Outside on the streets, workers were putting blue bulbs in the street lights, preparing for a black-out and to keep the city as dark as possible.

On September 3rd, 1939 when we came out of the morning service and returned home, we heard the news on the radio that German soldiers had marched into Poland. War was declared - the beginning of World War II. What was I to do?

At two o'clock one morning the sirens sounded out the air raid warning. Everybody was soon out of bed and about thirty of us went to the cellar with gas masks where we stayed for two and a half hours. Then the siren sounded for safety. There were air raid shelters everywhere. Isaiah 26:3* was very real to me during those days. My French studies were slowed up for a while, although my French teacher, Mlle Gindre, still stayed at the Institute and gave me lessons. Every morning I went down the street to buy milk and bread.

You will keep him in perfect peace, whose mind is stayed on You... NKJV

On the news, we heard the desolate state of the city of Strasbourg which is near the border of Germany. All 180,000 people had been evacuated. Then later on we heard that Warsaw was badly bombed. We covered all our windows with thick paper and even lights on cars were now painted blue.

During October, there were nights when we didn't get much sleep because of the heavy traffic passing along Grande Rue to the frontier. One could hear the soldiers marching on the cobble stones, then we heard the draught horses, hundreds of them that had been requisitioned by the military.

After spending seven and a half months in France, I returned to England in mid-November. My last letter home from France had in it the following poem:

His Name above all other names is glorious,
A place OF refuge in the day of strife;
To trust Him fully is to be victorious
In every hour and circumstance of life.
A verse from a poem by someone listed only as J. D. McK

When I arrived back at WEC Headquarters in London, I was told that I would be leaving for the Belgian Congo with Jack and Lily Roberts in about four weeks' time. Mr. Grubb, the head of the mission, was pleased that I had stayed in France for the extra two and a half months after war had broken out.

London during war time was dark. This made it more difficult for the German bombers to find their targets, and thus for me travelling by train to meetings it was difficult to find my station. I couldn't read the name of the station and had to just listen carefully to the conductor as he called out the names. The whole of London was dark.

At the weekend monthly conference at HQ, around one hundred people came and Mr. Grubb asked me to give my testimony and a farewell message. One chap who came to the conference brought me a pair of new shoes and another lady gave me three shirts and a pair of socks.

In spite of war, money for both advance work and existing work kept coming in to the Mission. Of course, we had prayed much for it, and God honours the prayer of faith.

Those days I was busy getting together my outfit to take to Congo. I had two steel trunks for my clothes, stationary and books. I had a box for hardware, kitchen utensils and books, as well as the two suitcases which I had brought from Australia. Then I had a bale with my camp cot, blankets, a folding trek chair, and a canvas bath tub. Folks at HQ packed and labelled my baggage, and sewed names on my clothes.

Before leaving I had one weekend at Nottingham, which was 138 miles north of London. One of the staff members asked me if I would take his place at their annual meetings and I was happy to do this. There I met one of the speakers, Mr. Jack Scholes, who later became our Field Director for the Congo field. I spoke at several meetings and at a lunch-hour meeting at a bicycle factory.

The last few days in England were taken up with getting shots, going to passport offices to obtain a permanent visa to stay in Belgian Congo and temporary visas to pass through France, Egypt, and Sudan. This was time consuming as these various offices were crowded with people. I was so glad to be getting away from London, because we had so much difficulty during wartime finding our way around in the dark, having to walk along the streets with a flash light.

Finally, the day came to leave for the Congo. Jack and Lily Roberts and I had a nice farewell at Victoria Station in London, then travelled to Newhaven where we caught the ferry to cross the English Channel to Dieppe. We crossed through France to Marseilles by train, then sailed from Marseilles across the Mediterranean in an Egyptian ship named El Nil (The Nile) to Alexandria, making one stop in Genoa, Italy. From Alexandria we took the three-hour train ride to Cairo.

The day we crossed the Mediterranean was Christmas Day and the Egyptian crew made a special Christmas dinner for the British people. That was nice and we appreciated it very much.

I was so glad to have the company of Jack and Lily Roberts who were just like a brother and sister to me. They were from a farm in Wales, a large family of fourteen made up of seven boys and seven girls, all Christians. Four of the girls were nurses and three were teachers.

Chapter 3

First Term
1940 to 1950

450 km to Khartoum

Juba

South Sudan

White Nile

Dingila   Niangara   Faradje   Aba

Albert Nile

Aru   Arua   Rhino Camp

Poko   Nala   Isiro   Watsa   Aru

Beta   Egbita   Gumba   Murchison Falls   Victoria Nile

Nebobongo   Rethy   Biriaba

Ibambi   Wamba   Masindi Port   Lake Kyoga

Bunia

Bomili   Mambasa   Nyankunde   Lake Albert   Uganda

Kondolole   Bafwapoko   450 km to Nairobi

Bafwasende   Oicha   Fort Portal   Kampala

Kisangani   Opienge   Beni   Kasese   Entebbe

Railway Line

Congo River   Lubutu   Democratic Republic of   Lake Victoria

Mulita   Congo   Tanzania

Lowa   Punia   Goma   Rwanda

Names are current as of 2011.
Some mission stations, towns or roads
may no longer exist.
One inch = 50 km (approx)

Ibambi

1940

I arrived in Africa at the end of 1939, December 27th. From the Egyptian port city of Alexandria, we travelled down the Nile, and at the start of the new year of 1940 we arrived in Khartoum, Sudan. My heart was full of praise to God for the wonderful things He had done for me that year. He had enabled me to learn the French language. He had opened my way to get out of France, and a short while later out of England during war-time. He enabled me to move out to Africa and brought me safely across land and sea to the Nile River.

After arriving in the port of Alexandria, we travelled by train to Cairo where we only stayed a few hours, then left on another train for Shellal, where we changed to a river steamer. This was more pleasant than on the crowded train and the heat. Along the shores of the Nile from time to time we saw crocodiles and the Captain of the boat would often shoot at them. We also saw elephants, antelopes and hippos.

When we arrived at Wadi Halfa, which is the border between Egypt and the Sudan, we changed back to train again and travelled twenty-four hours to arrive in Khartoum. This was the worst train ride I ever had in my life. It was desert all the way. It was hot. The train rattled along at fifteen miles per hour. If it went faster it would stir up too much sand. Sometimes we had to close the windows and then we would nearly suffocate.

We stayed in Khartoum with an Ethiopian Christian man for ten hours. He represented the Bible Society in the Sudan. We left Khartoum at 6 pm and travelled by train again until 6 am next morning. Then we changed again to river steamer and barges; the steamer was pushing four barges in front and pulling three more behind. The name of this place was Kosti. This river steamer would take twelve days to go up river from Kosti to Juba. Along this part of the Nile we saw the Dinka tribespeople and passed by two SIM* mission stations.

* Sudan Interior Mission

We arrived at Juba in southern Sudan on Friday, January 12, 1940. One of our missionaries was there to meet us with a van and we then drove the 240 miles to the Congolese border, with three flat tires en route. After crossing the border, getting through customs without any difficulty, we were finally in the Belgian Congo. There was a mission station just across the border called Aba, belonging to the Africa Inland Mission, and here we were invited to stay the night.

The WEC mission truck was waiting in Aba for us, so the next day we set out for one of our stations called Niangara. We stayed with the missionaries that were there for the week-end.

On Monday, we set off for Ibambi, the mission station that was WEC's headquarters in the Congo, arriving on January 15th, 1940. We received a great welcome from both the missionaries and the local Africans upon arriving. Our field leader, Mr. Jack Harrison, was visiting another station, so we didn't meet him until a week later.

I spent a little over a year here at Ibambi before I was assigned to a mission station way down south called Lubutu.

The task before most missionaries when they first arrive on the mission field is to learn the language of the people. I started learning the Kiswahili language right away. Mr. Harrison was my teacher and I would spend seven to eight hours a day on language study. The Kiswahili language is spoken in eastern Belgian Congo as well as in other parts of East Africa.

I was so happy to have arrived at the place God wanted me. I had the assurance that this was God's will for my life. I liked Ibambi.

Every evening at 7 pm all the missionaries on the station would meet in the field leader's home for a time of fellowship and prayer. Mr. Harrison would read a portion of scripture and make some comments on the passage. If there was any news of our fellow workers from the other eleven stations then this would be given; then we would all pray around. It has been the custom on all our mission stations to do this. Prayer with our fellow missionaries each day is very important and binds you together and unity is strength. We met with the nationals for prayer at other times.

As I was leaving my first prayer meeting at the Harrison's place with others, someone called out "Nyoka!" (*snake*). We each were carrying our kerosene lanterns and watched the reptile being pounded to death. There were five snakes killed around our house the first month. Some were black mambas six to seven feet long: horrible creatures!

The first six months at Ibambi was routine with formal language study, and informal study - going out to villages on Sundays with a missionary and listening. When I was asked to speak, someone had to interpret for me. There were always odd jobs to be done around the station such as making shelves for the print shop, or helping to bind books that were printed there.

Mail came irregularly because of the war in Europe, and most letters had been opened en route and sealed up again.

A missionary couple who were interested in treating the lepers in the area asked me and another single fellow to go with them a few miles north of Ibambi and measure out a concession for them. The government had agreed for them to start a medical station. We first had to cut away the undergrowth and some small trees so that we could make a straight line of stakes. Eventually we had the four sides measured correctly. The new mission station was named Nebobongo. From that day in March, 1940 it grew into the busy medical centre that it is today.*

* Aubrey couldn't have guessed then in 1940, that his early surveying of this new hospital site would result in a thriving medical centre where his wife would give birth to their fourth child some eighteen years later.

During July of 1940, I was invited to spend four weeks with my Australian friend Harold Williams. I knew him when I was a boy as he had lived in Bendigo at one time. He was now 38 years of age and I was about ten years younger. Harold wanted me to accompany him during most of July to go to an unreached area in the Wamba district. I learned so much from

Harold, how he preached and taught the Africans. He gave me good advice on how to deal with Africans and how to win them to the Lord.

HAROLD WILLIAMS WAITS ON A FERRY FOR AUBREY, 1940

AUBREY WITH HIS BICYCLE IN A DUGOUT CANOE BEING POLED ACROSS A RIVER NEAR BOMILI, CIRCA 1944

Three Treks and Lubutu

1940 to 1941

The purpose of the trek with Harold was twofold: to visit a tribe south of Wamba where no Protestant missionary had been before, in search of a village to place a native teacher, and secondly, to visit the outlying churches and preaching places in the Wamba area.

Harold and I were accompanied by Musa and Danga, two local teachers, and we started out in a Ford car from Wamba on July 4th, 1940. This car had been owned by C.T. Studd, the founder of our mission, and he had bought it in Nairobi the year he died, 1931.

July 4

We left at 3 pm and drove for three hours towards Stanleyville. En route, we passed several preaching places and stopped to greet the Christians at each place. At the end of the day, we arrived in Batuka where there was a big mine with some 800 men working and about thirteen whites living there*. This place had a very keen church with a native pastor in charge who was a real man of God and a very gifted preacher. We unpacked our things in a room at the back of the church and then had our evening meal.

* *Probably the Kilo gold mine which operated from 1903 until it was nationalized in 1967.*

55

July 5
We had a morning meeting at 7 am in the church which was attended by thirty-five women and twelve men. After the meeting, Harold went to bed with fever and flea bites and we learned afterwards that the pastor kept his dogs in this place, so that accounted for the lively time we had with those wretched insects. My job then became that of a nurse and in between times I studied Kingwana (a Kiswahili dialect) In the evening we had a good meeting around the fire just outside the church. Harold had rather a bad night.

July 6
Another good meeting was held at 7 am. Harold was a little better and got up a little later in the day. The two back tires were flat so we got to work and found a nail in each. While mending these, we had a visit from a white man who was surveying the area*. Harold was well enough to take the evening meeting and after it finished, we interviewed the candidates for the baptism being held on the following day.
* This person was probably surveying the mine concessions, showing the actual boundaries of the mining territory that were being given to the company by the government.

July 7
This is Sunday and seventy people come to the early morning service. Another service followed at 11 am after which we went down to the water where three men were baptized, the first ever at this place. One of these men hopes to soon go into the evangelistic school at Ibambi. At 2 pm, we held another service and after that one, a marriage. Following the evening meal, we went for a walk and then came back to sit around the fire, sing some hymns, and listen to testimonies. Harold gave his testimony and then made an appeal. One woman responded and received Christ as her Savior.

July 8
Before the next morning's meeting, we had breakfast and then packed up, leaving at 9:30 for our next stop - a tribe of people who had not yet been visited by missionaries. The chief of these people received us very favorably and showed us a house in which we could stay. We put out some of our books for sale

and sold quite a few that afternoon. In the evening, two white men stopped at the village so we visited with them, and they invited us to listen to the news on their radio. This was a treat, to be able to get news directly even though we were way out in the bush.

July 9
Today another white man arrived from Wamba and brought us supplies and mail. All was welcome. We spent the day in the chief's village and in the evening had a meeting outside the place where we are staying. Not many listened. There were three believers in this village who came along many times for teaching. They were the result of a visit from one of our teachers a few months ago.

July 10
Today it rained up to midday. When it stopped raining, we packed up to start off on a fortnight's *(two-week)* trek around the chief's territory. We left the car in a shed where the chief keeps his car and truck. Seven porters carry our belongings from one village to the next, where they change and another seven men carry them the next day to the next village. We left the chief's village at 2 pm and walked for three hours along a track through dense forest. Not a house to be seen until we arrived at the village. Most of these villages are small with a road down the center and about a dozen houses on both sides with each village having a man in charge. The head man in this village welcomed us and showed us a place to sleep and arranged for some food to be brought to us. We had a meeting at night around the fire. The folks seemed a bit scared; some stayed for a while but then ran off. Nobody responded in this place.

July 11
Harold and I spent the day in this village. On the next day the men of the village were going hunting, so they arranged a dance in the evening. Their belief is that a dance the night before a hunt will bring them great success the following day. But the noise of the drums and the people yelling was deafening, so Harold went out and asked them to stop as we needed

to sleep. A few minutes later, all was quiet and we went to sleep.

July 12
Early in the morning, the hunters had their long nets outside. They come out and formed a ring around the nets. One man in the center had a mug of water and sharp arrow. He went to each man and cut his tongue with the arrow and gave him a mouthful of water; then the men spit their blood and water over the nets. They believed this will make the nets strong and give them good success in the forest. On our return trip we learned they had a very poor day of hunting, so we told them all their superstition was of no help to them. It is dreadful to see how superstition binds these folks. We passed on to the next village six miles away, and in the evening had a meeting; not many listened.

July 13
Had breakfast; packed up and left for the next village, three hours walk. Visited with the people and had a good meeting in the evening. Almost the whole village turned out to hear the message.

July 14
Today is Sunday, but of course, Sunday doesn't mean anything to these people and early in the morning they go off to work in their gardens the same as any other day. We had a service at 10 am for those who remained in the village and then had an interesting talk with an old man who was a Muslim, yet didn't know much about his religion. On this trek we met quite a number following the Muslim religion. Two men made a profession of faith at the evening meeting.

July 15
We passed on to the next village three hours away and had a good meeting in the evening.

July 16
Today, after an hour and a half of walking we reached the furthest point of our trek where we had a good meeting in the evening. One man makes a profession of Christ. In the evening

we noticed thousands of driver ants coming for our house, so some of the porters put hot coals on the ground which turned them away and we enjoyed a peaceful night.

July 17
Heavy rain began at 5 am and delayed our departure until 10:30. After a short service we began the return journey. We walked four and a half hours. En route we saw a lot of large reddish monkeys* jumping across the tops of the tall trees. This was a very interesting break in the journey.
*These were probably Red Colobus monkeys, of which there are several species.

July 18
After we met with and instructed the four believers in this village, we continued on and walked another five hours before we arrived back at the first village we came to after leaving the chief's village.

July 19
We branched off to the left (east) from here and visited a few more new villages on our way back to the chief's. The first village was two hours away where we stayed the night and there was no response from the two meetings we held there.

July 20
A four-hour walk today led us to a place where we stayed the week-end. The people in this village were more interested in their dancing than the gospel message.

July 21
Had a Sunday morning service and not many listened. Most of the village people had left just after daybreak. After breakfast we scattered out and taught in the small nearby villages. A man and a boy came to get right with God near evening.

July 22
Heavy rain set in early but it cleared around 10 am and we were able to leave. After an hour we came to a flooded river with no sign of the fallen tree that we had previously used as a bridge. So, we waded in and just over half way across, the cur-

rent proved too strong and I was swept off my feet. Splash! Fortunately, I could swim and was soon on the other side and waited for the safe arrival of Harold and the others. Praise God for such a deliverance. All I lost was a pencil. After a further two-hour walk, we reached our destination and had our usual evening meeting. We had a good number of people at the start, but most of them fled during the service. Three old men are believers in this village.

July 23
After a two-hour walk we finally arrived back at the chief's village. Harold arranged with the chief about putting a teacher amongst his people and he was quite willing and named two villages.

July 24
All aboard the car today and we left the chief and his village and headed to another outlying church a few miles further on along the Stanleyville road. With all the recent rain, one of the big rivers was flowing fast and it took us two and a half hours to cross. This river is between ten to twelve chains wide (66 feet = 1 chain or 200 metres) and flows very fast. Seven men had to go over in a canoe to fetch the 'bac'* for us to go across on. There are very few bridges out here. We had to cross this same river about an hour later and this time we went across in a half hour as the bac was handy and more men were on the job. I stayed at this outlying church with one of the teachers while Harold and the others went on to another preaching place for the night.
* Modern flat-bottomed ferries powered by diesel engines would had been installed at the crossing points of the larger rivers by the mid to late 1940s, but the smaller crossing points would still have been serviced by a tradition-al ferry or bac. These were made of several pirogues (local dugout canoes) made from hollowed-out tree trunks and tied together with a platform of planks in the middle upon which the vehicle would be driven. The bacs were either poled across, if the river was not very deep, or pulled across by a cable or rope that had been stretched across the river.

July 25
Harold returned back at 10 am and we spent the day at this same place. The teacher in this village was away evangelizing in the district and had a very fine work going on here. It was

started by a native evangelist about three years ago. Harold and I went to another preaching place nearby for the evening service where the people have just started building a church.

July 26
After the morning service we left for the mines again at Batuka. At the river, we stayed for an hour or two helping a Congolese driver to get his lorry *(truck)* loaded with potatoes out of the mud. It had slipped off the ramp as he was driving onto the bac. People passing gave us news of the European war situation for which we were longing to hear after being away for over a fortnight without any news of the outside world. A Belgian asked us out for supper and we had an opportunity to witness.

July 27
After the morning meeting we went to another mine about eight miles through the forest. At this place we were kindly entertained by a Belgian couple. About 250 men worked here and we had two services, one Saturday evening and one Sunday morning. About seventy people attended. This work had just started and those interested wanted to build a church. That night we killed a scorpion in our bedroom.

July 28
After dinner we left for Batuka again, and arrived in time for the afternoon service. At night we had a prayer meeting around the fire outside the church.

July 29
We now turned towards home and spent one night at a little preaching place that had just started. Soldiers working on a bridge nearby came up and bought some books in the evening.

July 30
After breakfast we had another meeting with these folks. Three signify that they wanted to get right with God at the meeting. We then left and came to another mine just off the main road. One of our teachers was working here and he had just finished building a church. We made the church our place of lodging

during our stay with these folks. About sixty people came to the meeting that night.

July 31

Today we returned to Wamba after having a good meeting. One backslider came back to the Lord; praise God for all His goodness and blessing.

After I did this month-long trek in July, I did two more treks before Christmas, one was by myself accompanied by an African teacher. It was three weeks without speaking English and during those three weeks I didn't see another white person. I was just beginning to speak in Kiswahili and it was good practice to preach twice a day.

The next trek was for nearly two months and this time it was with another missionary named David Davies. I bought a Belgian-made bike and we did this trek together on our bicycles. We went ninety miles south-west from Ibambi to preach amongst the Babari people. Some places we had trouble to get porters to carry our boxes, but many souls were saved on this trek.

Towards the end of the year we got word from Mr. Harrison that he wanted us to return. There had been an urgent call from the Niangara missionaries for someone to come and help them take meetings amongst an invasion of Congo soldiers who were living in military camps near the mission there. These soldiers were from different parts of Congo, and were on their way north to help the Ethiopians in their fight against the Italians.*

* When Mussolini's Italy sided with Germany in World War II, the Belgians sent a force of Congolese soldiers up through Sudan to what was then called Italian East Africa. They joined the British and other African countries to help the Ethiopians defeat the colonial Italians. Italy's brief attempt at colonization lasted from 1935 to 1941.

David and I were glad to go. He knew Bangala, the language spoken up there, and I helped to sell literature while learning Bangala. Some of these soldiers were Christians and attended the meetings.

It was here at Niangara that the four of us single men spent Christmas, my first Christmas in Congo.

Early in the New Year of 1941, the soldiers moved on, and after six weeks in Niangara, David and I returned to Ibambi.

On March 6th, 1941, Mr. Harrison the field leader, took me and my baggage in his van from Ibambi to Opienge. I was assigned to a station even further south than Opienge, called Lubutu. In those days there was no motor road to Lubutu, so the journey had to be on foot from Opienge to Lubutu. It took me fourteen days of trekking to get there.

Mr. Ivor Davies, who was stationed at Opienge at that time, kindly lent me fifteen of his workmen to carry my things. He came with me for part of the long journey. I sent seven of the men carrying my things on ahead and I came on behind with the other eight porters.

The reason for this was that in the villages where we camped for the night, the folks would hear the message we gave them twice instead of just once. Then too, to find accommodation and food was better this way. We journeyed for hours through dense forest without seeing a village one day.

When we finally arrived at Lubutu, we received a great welcome from the Christians there. The men rested up for a few days and after I paid them, they returned to Opienge.

Mr. Harold Coleman and Mr. and Mrs. Colin Buckley were the missionaries on this station. Colin and Ina invited me to eat meals with them and this started a friendship that lasted for decades.

One village we stayed at coming in from Opienge and near to Lubutu, was so responsive that it was suggested I return there. I went back to this village of Tobinga and started a regular meeting in front of the headman's house at 6:30 every morning. At 9 am I would teach thirty children the 3Rs. They returned at 2 pm for more school, and in the evening, I would preach again when the adults had returned from their gardens. Several of the village people became Christians and a church was built. Later, a Christian school was put up for the children.

The year of 1941 was spent in trekking, church planting and station work, where I had to supervise the twenty-two workmen on the station. Most of the men were believers and they attended school as well as working part time.

In August, Mr. Buckley needed treatment for dysentery so I took him in his truck to the Lualaba River, where he caught the river steamer and then the train to Stanleyville. Twelve miles downriver from there was the Baptist Mission Hospital. Mr. Buckley was there for three weeks, then returned to Lubutu but in a few weeks he had to go back for further treatment.

In September, the missionaries who had opened up this new station returned from their furlough in Britain. They were Mr. and Mrs. Jim Grainger with their two-year-old son David.

With the arrival of the Graingers, we were now five missionaries at Lubutu and it was suggested I go out into the forest and preach in the villages. This is the work I loved. I arranged to have a good interpreter to go with me and a few believers to carry my boxes. We arranged a circular tour and we asked the Lord that one hundred souls would be saved on this seven-week trek. We started out and it was hard going. We got opposition from the Roman Catholics as they had already put their teachers in some of these villages.

As we got further along, people became interested and began to respond. I preached twice a day and we visited thirty-one villages in those seven weeks and there were over a hundred who expressed a desire to follow Christ and leave their heathen ways. Many had never prayed to God before. When I asked them to ask God's forgiveness they would say, "I don't know how to". Then I would pray and they would repeat the sinner's prayer after me.

At one place where I camped for the night, the villagers were beating drums and dancing. It was a terrible noise. Around 10 pm I went to them and asked them to stop as I wanted to sleep. They didn't take any notice and kept on. At midnight I went again. I walked right up to the drummers and took three or four of the skin-covered drums, returned to my hut and put them under my camp cot. Then I went to sleep. The next morning some men came meekly to the door and said, "Eh Bwana, can we have our drums back?" So, I returned the drums to them.

A growing problem at Lubutu was that we lacked trained teachers. With such a good response to the gospel in the area, the need was great for teachers. God called some of the believers to come to the station so that we could upgrade their education, make sure of their suitability and then send them on to Bible School supported by the church. When they graduated, they became pastors and evangelists. With God's help, they have done a good job, as reports we received in the 1980s -

some forty years later - said that around 6000 believers were gathering at Lubutu for their annual Christmas conferences.

In April of 1942, word reached us down at Lubutu that a Field Conference for all the Congo missionaries was to be held in June at Ibambi. I went along, hitchhiking with the Graingers. We travelled by truck, river boat, train and then by trucks again to reach our head station. At one place, the captain of the river steamer would not let us get on, so we had to wait another four days for the next boat. We arrived four days late for Conference. It was great to meet all the forty-seven missionaries and seventeen children; many of them I had not seen before. Mr. Harrison's messages on Ephesians were an encouragement to me.

During the business sessions at this conference, it was decided that a mission station which had been abandoned because of lack of personnel, should be reopened. Three men were chosen to go there. Mr. Fred Dunbar, whose wife had recently died at Ibambi, Cliff White, recently out from Britain, and I, made up the team.

After the conference, I returned to Lubutu and packed up. It had been a happy sixteen months that I spent there but it was time for my next assignment. I was taken to Wamba, where Harold Williams drove me and my belongings through Bomili and as far west as we could go, to where the road ended. From there, I asked the chief for twenty-five porters to carry my baggage* on the two-day trek to the station known as Kondolole.

While it does seem like a lot of luggage that necessitates twenty-five men to carry it all, it was not just his clothes and shaving kit that he paid porters to carry. How many pairs of khaki shorts and safari jackets can one man have?

Actually, his entire outfit that he would have brought from England, would have gone with him to each mission station to which he was sent, allowing him to be as self-sufficient as possible. The outfit would have included his camp cot, mosquito netting, bedding, a folding table and chair, a canvas bath tub, a small medical kit, several books, writing materials, some tools, and a small kitchen trunk containing a kettle, a few pots, plates and cutlery, and some basic foodstuffs like flour, rice, powdered milk, tinned biscuits, tea and sugar. And yes, several pairs of khaki shorts, safari jackets, knee-high socks and a pith helmet - pretty much the uniform for expatriates working in the tropics well into the 1950s.

# # # # #

Deuteronomy 31:8 *The Lord, He it is that doth go before thee; He will be with thee, He will not fail thee, neither forsake thee: Fear not, neither be dismayed.*

Did I prove these promises to be true? I surely did. As each year before us is an unknown path, we can rely on our Guide and His promises.

This is my testimony as I reflect upon the faithfulness of God from 1940 to 1951 which was my first term of service in the Belgian Congo. I want to summarize briefly the places where I had the privilege of ministering during these eleven years.

Ibambi, 13 months. After learning the Kiswahili language, I did the three treks mentioned above where I preached to many.

Opienge, 2 weeks. In 1942, I was at Opienge for two weeks on the station and then trekking through part of that territory on my way to Lubutu.

Lubutu, 6 months. Here I did a lot of trekking and church planting work.

Kondolole, 30 months. In this area among the Babari tribe, I planted churches over a large area.

Niangara, 3 years, 8 months. It was hard going here as there was strong opposition from the Roman Catholics. I did a lot of trekking and taught in a school for boys.

Nala, 24 months. I was married here at the end of 1948, and continued working mainly on the station until our furlough in early 1951.

Being a single missionary for eight and a half years, I could easily be moved wherever there was a need. I was grateful to God for the experience of seeing and working with several devoted missionaries and nationals in various places of the WEC area, as well as learning two languages, Kiswahili and Bangala.

On Trek, 1940

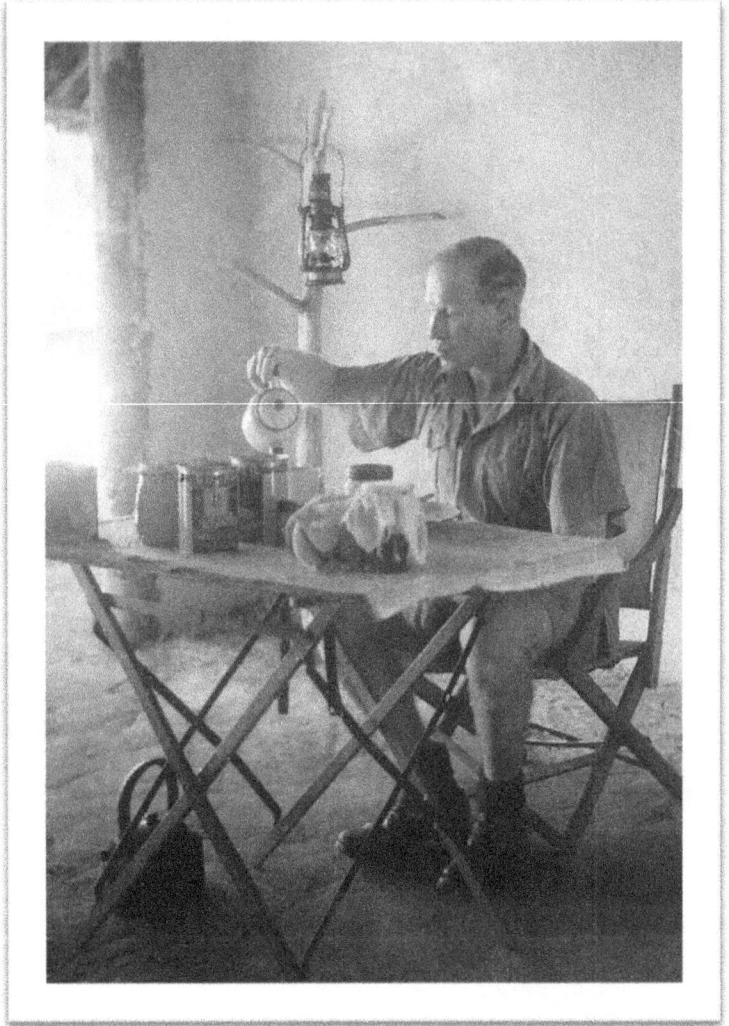

TEA TIME FOR AUBREY, 1943

Kondolole and Niangara

1942 to 1948

Kondolole, two years and six months

I arrived at Kondolole mission station on August 11, 1942. The main tribe in this area was the Wabari people who spoke Kiswahili. Here I joined two fellow missionaries, Fred Dunbar and Cliff White.

After we had been together for a while it was decided that Cliff and I should move out into the villages, and Fred would do the station work. Later on, Cliff started a boys' school and village churches came into being. God was working in the hearts of these Wabari people.

One day I came across a coffee plantation. I went in to see who was there. There was a Belgian man with his wife and six children, three boys and three girls. They invited me in for a meal. They didn't know English so we conversed in French. This plantation owner had 200 tons of coffee stored, but could find no way to have it transported to market as it was war time in Europe.

Back on the station, Fred was re-roofing two of the missionary houses with shingles. We had a conference at Christmas but it was not well attended. At the business meeting, a goal was set to visit every village in our area with the gospel in the coming year, 1943.

Both 1943 and 1944 were good years, spent mostly in church planting and establishing schools. At one point we received news that Harry Jones, the missionary who had pioneered this work at Kondolole and was on furlough in England, was making plans to return - only now he was not a single man anymore. He had found a wife and this was exciting news that they would be soon with us at Kondolole. Meanwhile Fred had to leave and attend to his young son. Mrs Harold Williams had been looking after the motherless boy at Wamba and now it was Fred's time for furlough. He left with his son for England.

A few details are not mentioned here: Fred Dunbar's wife, Val died in early 1942 and their young son stayed with Mrs. Williams at Wamba, while Fred was sent to Kondolole with the two bachelors. Mrs. Harold (A. McNeil) has not been mentioned, but it seems Harold was married when Aubrey met and trekked with him.

It was here at Kondolole that I started getting boils on my arms and legs. At times they were so painful that I had to be carried to places to preach. At last, I sent for help and a car was sent down from Ibambi to take me to where I could get medical attention. Our nurse and a Belgian doctor treated me and soon, eating better food than we had at Kondolole, I was feeling much better. After a few weeks I was able to return to my work.

The pioneer missionary, Harry Jones and his new wife Gladys arrived from England. It was good to see them. Harry and Gladys invited Cliff and I to come over to their home and eat meals with them when we were back on the station after our treks. This was refreshing.

While I was out in the area among the people preaching and teaching, I was gathering up boys for the station school. I had twenty-nine travelling with me at one point. After a while, it was getting difficult because I had to buy food for all the boys, so I decided to hasten back to the mission station and hand them over to Cliff. The boys' school now had eighty elementary students.

In one village near the Lindi river where I was teaching, they had just witnessed a very sad event. One of the village women was attacked by a crocodile and killed. There was a lot of sickness in the village; some had leprosy and others were inflicted with yaws and tropical ulcers with little medicine available.

70

We thanked the Lord many times for His protection from harm and danger and disease. Occasionally we were pestered with jiggers burrowing into our feet and laying their eggs there, if we failed to remove them in time. The Congolese were good at digging them out of our feet.

In a rest house* where I was staying while out in a village, two Indian traders came and stayed in the other vacant room. I was able to give them two chickens that I had purchased from the natives. When they were leaving, they gave me tea, macaroni, a bottle of cherries, pickles, tinned fish, corned beef and half a loaf of bread. They were returning to civilization and could buy more food there. Can God furnish a table in the wilderness? He surely can!

*Rest houses were small public guest houses scattered throughout a colony, usually two empty rooms with a hall down the middle where up to two people could stay on each side. Administrators, traders and missionaries would travel in remote areas and would need a place to stay, so these fit the bill. Although they were far from comfortable, they at least provided a roof and some privacy. In the early days they were just earthen walls and floor with a grass roof, but eventually were constructed of brick walls, concrete floors and tin roofs.

Early in 1945, Cliff and I were given new assignments, so we packed our belongings and were ready when the mission truck arrived at Kondolole. The motor road had been finished and passed by our station. We returned to Ibambi ready for another assignment. Our work in the Wabari area was now finished after spending approximately two and a half years among these people.

Kondolole had been a lonely place to live. We had no vehicle and we often went months without receiving mail. It was so isolated that it was difficult to purchase food apart from what we could buy from the Congolese.

I left this area with a growing church which was helped by missionaries and nationals. Kondolole eventually became a national church, being run entirely by the Congolese.

Years afterwards, another mission station was opened near Bomili and was named Buambi.

Niangara, three years and eight months

I arrived at Niangara on March 7th, 1945. My co-worker was David Davies, with whom I had done a two-month trek during my first year. Niangara is situated on the Uele river, 140 miles north of Ibambi and 200 miles south of the Sudanese border. Niangara was a government post with Belgian administrators and there was a bank and some shops owned by Greeks. Just outside the township was a large Roman Catholic mission where some twenty priests and nuns ran large schools and a seminary.

By comparison, the Protestant mission and work was very small and insignificant. We were ridiculed by the Catholics and received much opposition. However, we were not ashamed of the gospel of Christ. There was little to see from the work of previous missionaries in the area.

Niangara had been the original station for the Heart of Africa Mission where Studd and Buxton started out, before they eventually settled on Ibambi, as the headquarters for the Congo field.

In this area we used the Bangala language to minister to the two main tribes which were Bazande and Mangbetu. Both of these tribes had a custom that when a baby was born, the baby's head was bound with course string and left on the head for a year or so and then the head would be elongated like the parents. It was a cruel ordeal for little ones. Truly they were in heathen darkness.

At Niangara, there was now a 1931 Chevrolet car which the missionaries had bought from a Congolese chief. This made trekking much easier and faster. David and I took turns trekking, with one of us out in the area and the other on the mission station.

On May 5th, our field leader, Jack Harrison died. He had preached on the Sunday and the next day he had pain so was taken to the doctor at Wamba, 50 miles from Ibambi. Early the following day his earthly journey was over. He was 45 years of age. Harold Williams drove by car from Ibambi to Niangara to pick up David and me and then we went to Poko to tell the missionaries there and from there we left for Ibambi arriving at 2 am. The funeral was that day. Crowds of Congolese came as Mr. Harrison's body was laid to rest in Ibambi alongside the grave of C.T. Studd. Twenty-two missionaries were at the funeral; others were too far away to come.

At the end of May, a field conference was called to elect a new leader. Mr. Jack Scholes was chosen which meant he had to leave Poko and move to Ibambi.

The Buckleys, who had been at Lubutu when I was there, returned to Congo after three years at home because of health reasons. They were now assigned to Niangara. David and I were happy they came to join us. They took on the station work, I supervised the boys' school and David did the trekking.

When the school was on a holiday break, I was able to do village work. It was hard work. In many places the people wouldn't gather for a meeting as they feared the Roman Catholic teachers. We had to contact the people while they were working in their gardens and give the gospel to them one by one.

In this northern part of Congo, it is grassland instead of forest. When I arrived at one village, they had just killed a lion. No one would go out of their houses after dark as it was too dangerous with lions and leopards prowling around. Elephants also roamed in the area and destroyed the gardens of the Africans. In the Uele river we would often see hippos and crocodiles.

Towards the end of 1946 I got sick with dysentery. I received injections of emetine from the local hospital and after tests the doctor said I was free from the sickness.

As the tires and tubes of our car were worn out and there was no way of purchasing any new ones in the Congo, we were restricted somewhat from going long distances into the area to preach. We received an evangelist from Ibambi to help in the village work and one from Nala as well.

At Niangara we could get better food than at Kondolole. We could buy fresh meat and vegetables, and fruit was plentiful.

During the years of 1947 and 1948, I spent a lot of time trekking in the large area of the Niangara territory. In comparison with Kondolole, where a hundred or more people lived together in one village and were easy to reach, the people of the Niangara lived in separate houses dotted throughout the grassland and some were so hidden away they were hard to find. Sometimes I would spend five weeks, sometimes three, preaching and teaching and doing personal work. The people were beginning to know us and were beginning to show interest and some churches were established, but it was slow going.

When I was having my evening meal alone on May 23rd, I had to shut all the doors and windows because I was invaded with a swarm of flying ants. The light from the pressure lamp had attracted them so I removed the lamp outside on the verandah. The house boy* was happy about that; he started gathering them up in handfuls and put them into a basin and put the lid safely on. Then later he would eat them. These flying ants live in mud ant-hills sometimes six feet high.** When it rains, and after dark, they start flying around. Their wings drop off and the Africans go out and gather them up for eating.

* *House boy was a term common throughout the colonial world used to describe a local person who was hired as domestic help for an expatriate. Laundry, cleaning, cooking, gardening, and child care were the common tasks. It provided much needed employment for locals and helped the expats deal with life in a developing country often without electricity, plumbing, or nearby stores. They also provided help understanding local culture and language.*
** *Both ants and termites produce flying versions of themselves as part of their reproductive cycles where they leave the colony once or twice a year when the temperature and humidity reach a certain point.*

On November 28th, I wrote home and announced to my folks about my engagement to Miss Hulda Schroeder, whom I had met at Nala the previous year. Hulda was a Canadian and had obeyed the Lord's call to come to Congo. She was assigned to Nala mission station to supervise and teach in the boys' school. Sometimes during school holidays, she went into the area visiting churches and schools.

In typical Aubrey fashion, he gives no details as to how they met. In Hulda's 2001 book, River of Memories, she fills in the picture.

"It was 1947, and the Congo was still under Belgian rule. Plans were underway for Prince Charles of Belgium to visit, and every effort was being made to make this a special occasion...The day's program was filled with performances of many kinds from native dances to athletic events. Witch doctors and chiefs showed up in their most colorful outfits, making it an interesting day of African culture ...It was at this occasion that I first met an Australian named Aubrey Brown, who had come down from his mission station to see the festivities and meet the Prince. I did not know it at the time, but I would get to know this Australian prince much better than the Belgian...After our short meeting, we started to correspond, and soon there came a letter of proposal for marriage...A few months later, he stopped at Nala for a two-day visit. It was a nice time of getting to know each other, but apart from that one visit, our courtship was mainly by correspondence due to the distance between our two stations...I had not come out to Africa to get married, and when the marriage proposal came, I battled with the decision for weeks. Perhaps the reason was that I did not know much about this man, and there was little opportunity to learn. The things I had learned about him were positive. He was a gifted linguist, for he had learned the French language before coming out to Africa and since arriving had also acquired two African languages. He had been a bachelor, working for over seven years in Congo, busying himself with a lot of trekking and evangelizing. All these were indeed positive points, as far as I was concerned. I remember writing to my family in Canada to say that this man who had proposed to me was not tall, dark and handsome, but he had a heart of gold! ... So, I agreed to Mr. Brown's proposal."

The Christmas Conference in 1947 at Niangara had more people attend and two women were accepted to be baptized in the Uele River. This was the first time I had baptized anybody.

In April of 1948, the mission arranged for me to have a four week's holiday at Rethy on the eastern edge of Congo. Rethy was an Africa Inland Mission station 350 miles from Niangara and was situated 7000 feet above sea level. Some friends there had invited me to come and spend some time with them, as I had worked seven years and a few months without a break and was getting tired in the work, but not of it. The climate there was cold at times and such a welcome change. The mission paid for my stay at Rethy and offered to pay my travelling expenses, but the Lord had provided that in another way.

At Rethy, there was a school for missionaries' children. Forty-five attended with about twenty missionaries living on the mission station. There was a hospital and a printing shop. While at Rethy, I was asked to speak at both the Congolese boys' and girls' schools and took one Sunday morning service in their huge church.

All four of his children would attend this school in later years.

One day, I was invited to go along on a trip to Mount Ruwenzori (16,000 feet), at the foot of which there was a mission station.

Aubrey probably meant Mt. Stanley, the highest peak of the Ruwenzori range that divides Uganda and DRC. Called the Mountains of the Moon since ancient times and now called the Rwenzori range, these mountains are home to the mountain gorillas.

When I arrived back from my holidays, I found another missionary couple at Niangara. Now we were five, as David had left for furlough.

I was out trekking again now full of vip and vim. Coming across some local shops, I went in to see if there was something I hadn't seen before and to my surprise I saw on the shelves some tins of Australian corned beef and some tins of Australian cheese. This was way out in the grasslands, miles away from civilization!

The Lord was working in the hearts of some of the school boys at Niangara and I started a mid-week meeting with a dozen or so of these who wanted to follow the Lord. This was an encouragement in a hard place.

On September 1, Aubrey wrote to his family telling them about Hulda and sending a picture.

In November of 1948, a letter from the field leader informed me that a change was to take place. Things were lining up for our wedding. Difficulties and delays over legal papers were now being resolved. The mission advised me that after our marriage I would be joining the staff at Nala. Mr. Scholes told me that I had to be residing in Nala territory two weeks before the wedding and that he would be coming to Niangara to move me down to Nala on November 16th. Really it wasn't hard at all to pack up once again and move in the right direction.

Two verses of scripture sum up the years I spent at Niangara. They are Ecclesiastes 11:1 and 6. *"Cast your bread upon the waters, for you will find it after many days. In the morning sow your seed, and in the evening do not withhold your hand; for you do not know which will prosper, either this or that, or whether both alike will be good." New King James Version.*

AUBREY AND HULDA NEAR NALA, 1948

The Move to Nala and the Wedding

1948 to 1950

On arriving at Nala in mid-November 1948 to join the workers there, I was asked to supervise the workmen. They would attend an hour's bible study from 6:30 to 7:30 am, have breakfast and then work from 8 am to 2 pm. Then they would gather for two hours of school and I would stay with them and correct their lessons. Some of these men, after their education was upgraded, would go on to Bible School and become evangelists and pastors.

Mr. and Mrs. English were the two senior missionaries at Nala and there were also two single ladies. One of the single ladies was in charge of the girls' school and the other was in charge of the boys' school. This latter one was the lady I had come to Nala to marry.

We were waiting for a permit to marry, a paper from the British Consul in Leopoldville. At last it came and the date of December 2 was set for our wedding day. When that last legal paper came, word was sent to the field leader at Ibambi and a telegram to Colin and Ina Buckley at Niangara.

Our wedding day at Nala on December 2, 1948, was a day I will never forget. We were married three times, in three places and in three languages.

The state wedding was held at the government office in Paulis*. Mr. Buckley took Hulda and I in to town in the morning and Mr. Scholes, the field leader from Ibambi, met us there at 10 am. The legal ceremony took half an hour with the Belgian Administrator officiating in French. Mr. Scholes and Mr. English had to sign the wedding documents as witnesses as well as Hulda and myself.

* Paulis, now Isiro, was the largest town in the area, about 15 km south of Nala, 75 km north of Ibambi, and 145 km south of Niangara.

After all this was done, and the congratulations received from the government officials, we returned to Nala for the church wedding.

This wedding started just before midday and was conducted in the Bangala language. Hulda wore a blue crepe wedding dress which she had made, with a white veil, shoes and ribbon which were sent out from Canada by her sisters. Hulda carried a lovely bouquet of red roses which she picked from her flower garden the morning of the wedding. I borrowed a Palm Beach suit* from a fellow missionary who had worn it for his wedding a few years before.

* Palm Beach is both a brand name from 1922 and a cotton/mohair blend of cloth suitable for tropical suits.

Some two hundred Congolese were in the Nala church waiting. One missionary played on a little Estey organ* "Face to face with Christ my Saviour" while we were waiting for the bride to enter.

* The Estey Organ Company from Vermont, USA, made a portable version of their pump organ that folded up into a large suitcase for use by military chaplains and overseas missionaries.

Hulda was given away by the senior missionary of Nala station, Mr. English. Mr. Scholes married us in the Bangala language and spoke on the second chapter of John.

When the service was over and we were pronounced husband and wife, we left the church through a side entrance and outside to our surprise the pastors and evangelists had formed an arch with Bibles in their hands for Hulda and me to walk under. We had some photos taken, then made our way over to the senior missionary's house for the third and final service. This service was in English, and it was here that I gave the wedding ring to Hulda which had been sent out from Australia. This brief and hallowed service was followed by communion. Just eight of us missionaries were present.

At this service, Hulda sang with two other Canadian missionaries, Hulda Martens and Ruth Dyer, the song *From Prayer that Asks* of which the last verse is as follows:

Give me the love that leads the way,
The faith that nothing can dismay,
The hope no disappointment tire,
The passion that will burn like fire,
Let me not sink to be a clod,
Make me Thy fuel, Flame of God.
Amy Carmichael

At 3 pm, the Belgian Administrator from Paulis joined us for the wedding banquet. We had cold meats, salads and plenty of homemade cakes.

Mrs. English had made a three-tier wedding cake and Hulda cut the cake and shared pieces with the guests. Other pieces were later wrapped and sent to all our fellow missionaries who couldn't attend and even to our parents and relatives.

We received many nice and useful presents from our relatives and fellow missionaries to start up our new home together. Hulda gave me a brief case that her brother bought and sent out with a missionary who was coming our way.

We started off with family devotions, which we have kept all through the following years. The family that prays together stays together. We didn't go away for a honeymoon but went back to work the following day!

Nala station where we lived was situated behind a large coffee plantation owned by two Belgians. We had to pass through this plantation to reach the motor road that led to Paulis, approximately ten miles away.

We regularly sent a worker on a bike to Paulis to post letters and bring back our mail and provisions from the stores. There were about 250 Belgian and Greek people living in the central part of Paulis. The Greeks were the traders and owned shops on the main street. There was a railway station, a bank, a post office, a hospital, and administration offices. There was a large transport company and garage which employed many Africans. In the native part of town there were about 5000 Congolese living.

A few weeks after our marriage it was time to have our annual Christmas conference. At this conference people came to Nala mission station from the churches out in the area. There would be around one thousand people, mostly Christians, for three days of celebrating the greatest thing in their lives, which was to worship and adore the Savior of the world and have fellowship one with another. These were happy days. In some meetings the children from the various churches would recite the Christmas story as recorded in Matthew and Luke's gospels and then sing a Christmas carol. During the conference days, the unsaved were challenged to get right with God and some forty people made decisions to follow Christ.

When the conference was over, the school children went home to their villages for holidays, and Hulda and I went to a Rest House just outside of Paulis and spent the next few weeks there evangelizing in the native town close by.

We had two local evangelists to help us; people showed interest and there was a response. Later a mission station was opened here which I helped to measure out, and it was called Gamba. Through the years the work developed here and eventually the headquarters of the mission was moved from Ibambi to Gamba.

The school children were due back to Nala at the beginning of February, so Hulda and I packed up and returned there to prepare for another term of school and station work. We lived in a modest mud brick house with a palm thatch roof and earthen floor.

About this time there was a death at the coffee plantation from yellow fever, so we all had to have fresh injections against this disease.

Sad news reached us from Canada at the end of February. It was the news of the death of Hulda's brother, Bill, who died working on the Alaska Highway.

A letter we wrote home to our parents on June 22 contained good news. We were announcing to them that we were expecting a baby towards the end of the year.

Later in the year, one of our friends offered us her car to take Hulda to Wamba for the confinement. The Buckley's were now at Wamba, and Hulda could stay with them until the baby was born. I took Hulda to Wamba and returned to Nala. After a few weeks, I returned with a nurse from Ibambi. Her name was Muriel Harman, another Canadian. There were two Belgian doctors at Wamba, a husband and wife team. Dr. Parmentier was the one who treated me for dysentery when I was at Niangara.

Our first child was born on October 27, and we named him Ronald William Brown. He brought great joy into our home. Now we were three. When we got back to Nala, we had a child dedication service and Ronnie was dedicated to the Lord. At six months he weighed ten and a half pounds and was twenty-four inches long.

As the year drew to a close we prepared for another Christmas conference.

In 1950, there were several highlights. The International Secretary of WEC, Mr. Norman Grubb, came to visit the Congo field. He first did a tour of the southern stations, then he came up north to visit the Bangala-speaking people. In the central and southern part of the Congo, the people spoke Kiswahili. By this time I could speak in both languages.

Mr. Grubb was no stranger to the older people as at one time he was a missionary at Poko and in the early days he translated the New Testament into Bangala. Mr. Grubb married Pauline, the daughter of Mr. C.T. Studd, who had founded the mission back in the year 1913.

Mr. Grubb and Mr. Scholes visited Nala in March and stayed with us for eight days. These days were very refreshing for us as Mr. Grubb ministered the Word every evening as we missionaries met together after the day's work.

In April, there was field conference at Ibambi where Mr. Grubb was the main speaker. Fifty missionaries attended and we enjoyed the fellowship of our missionaries and the spiritual uplift. It was Ronnie's first conference. I don't know if he enjoyed it or not, but he sure got a lot of attention.

Later in the year, Pastor Sidlow Baxter from London, England, came to visit a former member of his congregation at Ibambi, Mrs. Harrison, who had lost her husband in 1946. This pastor and writer visited a few nearby stations, but we didn't meet him.

Ronnie, our son, was growing and doing well. At eight months old, his face would light up and he would chuckle when our house boy would bring the porridge to the table at breakfast time. At ten months he was beginning to stand up holding on to the side of his play pen. In October he had his first birthday party.

Hulda was busy with school work, supervising the Congolese school teachers from her office at home while looking after the little boy. I was with the workmen re-roofing the Nala church and other building projects. Sometimes I was able to stay with Ronnie while Hulda went to school. In November, Ronnie was vaccinated against smallpox and he didn't cry. His parents were proud of him.

At the end of the year of 1950, news came to us that my father was in hospital and dying from cancer. We started making preparations to leave for furlough, first to go to Australia.

I had been away from home and loved ones for thirteen years.

Chapter 4

First Furlough
1951 to 1952

HULDA, AUBREY, RONALD AND TWINS KEN AND CAROL IN BENDIGO, 1952

Australia and Canada

1951 to 1952

During the last week in January and the first week in February, Hulda and Ronnie were able to have a two-week holiday at another mission station called Poko. Hulda's two friends from Canada were working in that area and at the end of the holiday, they brought Hulda and Ronnie back to Nala. While Hulda was away, I was re-roofing Mr. English's house with the workmen.

News from home was that Dad was failing in health, so the Field Director arranged for us to leave for furlough on February 24th.

Mr. English loaned us his International truck and Mr. Grainger drove us to the Nile River. We left Nala early Friday morning and reached an African Inland Mission station at Aru by evening. The missionaries there, Austin Pauls and his wife, kindly took us in and gave us hospitality. The next day we crossed the border, passed through customs, and were now in Uganda. Then we drove the forty miles to Rhino Camp situated on the Nile River. Here we said goodbye to our beloved Jim Grainger and boarded the river steamer.

Reaching Lake Albert, we changed onto a lake steamer and crossed over to Butiaba. From here we had to take a bus to Masindi Port where we boarded another river steamer to take us across Lake Kyoga to a railway station. That train took us all the way to Nairobi and took 27 hours.

In Nairobi I bought a much-needed suit of clothes as for eleven years I had mostly been wearing shorts. After a short stay we made our way down the coast to Mombasa by train, where we bought our tickets on a ship bound for Colombo.*

* *Sri Lanka*

In Colombo, we found a ship bound for Melbourne, Australia. We stayed on this boat until we reached Perth, where we got off and took a plane in order to get to Melbourne faster. Our baggage stayed on the ship and we picked it up later when it arrived in Melbourne. At the airport in Melbourne, my brother Rupert and a WEC representative met us. And then, after a three-hour drive north by car, the long journey from Nala to Bendigo was over.

In the Maps section of the Blog, the scope of this trip can be seen in detail.

At 71 Bobs Street in Bendigo, we met my mother and sister Gladys, and my father who was very ill. He recognized me and we were able to talk together. How nice it was to be back home after an absence of thirteen years. Truly the Lord had watched over us while we were absent one from another.

After we had been home for a few weeks Dad passed away quietly at his home in Bendigo where we were staying. He was 78 and died of cancer. He was now home with the Lord and free from suffering. I was thankful that I had those last weeks with him. He was buried in the White Hills cemetery, near Bendigo.

Meeting relatives and friends over the next few days, and weeks, and months was somewhat strange. As for some, their hair had changed color and others, well wrinkles had begun to appear. What a difference thirteen years can make in a person's appearance!

Evelyn Dawe was a young lady that often dropped by to say hello on her way to work. It was nice to see her, although the attraction was not so much us who had returned from Africa, but there was interest in my younger brother.

In the month of August, Rupert and Evelyn were married in the White Hills Church, and made their home in Bendigo.

At this time, we were expecting our second child by the end of the year.

Deputation work while on furlough was something that I was not looking forward to. A mission society expects missionaries that are on furlough to visit churches and various groups of people, holding meetings and attending missionary conferences to speak of what God has been doing in faraway mission fields. This is an opportunity to challenge young people to totally commit their lives to Christ and to be available to Him for anything God may ask them to do. Interest can be stirred up in the hearts of the older people to pray without ceasing for the heathen, for lost souls, for new converts, for new churches to be established, and for the training of national leaders. Prayer can help in the granting of visas for missionary candidates ready to go out to needy lands.

But the thought of being separated from my wife and child for weeks at a time was something that I was not happy about. Being in a different home every night among strange people was going to be something different for me.

We had brought home a few photos from Africa, which were made up into glass slides and then coloured by hand. These would illustrate my talks at the meetings that had been arranged and away I went.

Once I got started, it wasn't as hard as I had imagined. Meeting people interested in the work missionaries were doing was encouraging.

It was a joy to tell them what we had seen God do in Africa in the years we had been there. What a story we had to tell! What a privilege it was to be His witnesses. I travelled with a good supply of missionary books and literature, which I displayed at meetings. I trusted that the books and literature taken would bear fruit after I had moved on to take further meetings. God can use the written message as well as the spoken word; He used both in calling me to Africa.

One does not always see results from deputation work. We leave that with God. One has to be willing to serve on the home end of a mission as well as on a mission field overseas.

In November of 1951, another tour had been arranged for me to take meetings, in north-eastern Victoria. My wife was pregnant and we were expecting an addition to our family in early December. The day I was due to leave we had made an appointment to see Hulda's doctor. The doctor said after examining her, "I can hear only one heartbeat, but I don't know what all these arms and legs are that I can feel!"

Hulda asked the doctor that if he thought there may be twins, she would like to know. The doctor said he could arrange for her to have an X-ray, and find out. We agreed for this and the X-ray revealed that instead of one baby coming, there were two on the way!! Hulda and I were so stunned that we did not say a word to each other on the way home! On arriving home Hulda stayed, and I loaded up the car, and started off for the first meeting of the tour about 80 miles away. I had planned a month's itinerary but was able to cancel some meetings and return earlier.

Carol and Ken were born in Bendigo Hospital and all went well. How wonderfully God provided for them and their mother in the hospital. A Christian doctor attended the birth. A lady that was unknown to us had just previously given birth to a baby. She had been the recipient of many generous gifts of baby's clothes, more than she could possibly use. She was a doctor and had heard that there was a mother in the hospital who had just given birth to twins. She graciously sent Hulda a good supply of baby clothes that she didn't need. Here again God supplied needs according to His word in Philippians 4:19. *But my God shall supply all your needs according to His riches in glory by Christ Jesus.*

In Australia, for many years, a convention of 2000 or more people, mainly Christians, was held every year the last week in December. The beautiful Convention Center was called Belgrave Heights and was situated in the forests east of Melbourne. I somehow was free to go and wanted to attend this year as I had been overseas for thirteen years. My brother offered his truck. His wife, Evelyn, and other relatives and friends expressed a desire to go to the convention also. We arrived at Belgrave Heights for the beginning of the meetings and what a blessed week we had! Good speakers, good fellowship! I had opportunities to share messages at a house party where I was invited to be their missionary guest. We returned to Bendigo with much joy for the blessings we received at the convention.

See the Belgrave Heights pamphlet in photo section of the blog.

On March 14th, it was time to say goodbye to family and friends in Australia and to cross the Pacific Ocean to Canada to meet Hulda's family. We left Melbourne with our three small children on a Norwegian ship, the M/S *Ventura*. It took us nineteen days to cross the Pacific. When we were nearing Los Angeles, we sent a telegram to our mission headquarters for someone to come and meet us on arrival. Sure enough, someone was there and took us thirty-five miles from the coast to headquarters where we stayed for a few days getting to know our home base leaders and some missionary candidates.

We left Los Angeles by train on April 7th and arrived in Canada two days later at Vancouver. Hulda's brother and sister* were there to meet us as well as some of their children and some of Hulda's friends. We stayed six days at each of the brother's place and the sister's place. It was nice to meet them and their families. While at Hulda's oldest brother's place, Hulda was able to contact her parents by phone and tell them we were now nearer home, only 1300 miles away by train. It was a big change for me to see the high Rocky Mountains and get used to Canadian life. It was April and springtime. The fruit trees were in blossom and there were acres of strawberries planted in British Colombia.

* *John and Suzie Schroeder, Elizabeth and Frank Peters*

Something I hadn't seen yet in my life was a hockey rink, which is a popular sport in Canada. It seemed everyone up from three and four years of age could skate on ice and many played hockey. In the summer the popular game was baseball.

After these two visits were over in British Columbia, we boarded the train to go east through the Rocky Mountains, then pass through the province of Alberta, and finally arrived on the prairies in Saskatchewan at a small town called Herbert. It was April 24th.

It was here in Herbert, where Hulda's parents and her older sister Emma lived. The parents had moved off their farm in Main Center, fourteen miles north, to retire in Herbert. As the train pulled to a stop in this small town early in the morning, I met for the first time my father-in-law, Mr. Isaac Schroeder and his wife, Gertrude, my mother in law. I also met three of Hulda's sisters and a brother-in-law. We forgot about our tiredness as we had travelled all night in the train and were relieved to know that our long journey was now over. What a welcome we received!

The three children were soon in the arms of their new aunties and were cared for. We were taken to the Schroeder home and there we rested up and relaxed. The Lord had safely brought us all the way with the little ones. The following days and weeks, relatives and friends kept dropping by to greet us and welcome us home.

Herbert is a farming community and in May the farmers were busy sowing their crops, mostly wheat and barley.

Right close to where we were staying there was a missionary conference scheduled for the first week in June. We were happy to hear that the main speaker was Dr. Oswald Smith and his messages were a blessing and challenge to me. I had been asked to share some news of our work in Congo one evening and it was an honor for me to be sitting with Dr. Smith on the platform. It was a good conference and well attended. At the close a pledge offering was taken for missions amounting to much more than everyone expected.

For two weeks I was able to go out to Hulda's brother's place on a ranch.* He had moved a house on to the yard where he and his wife lived. They needed to build a concrete cistern in the basement and a concrete floor as well, so I was able to help a little.

Abe and Lydia Schroeder

During that summer another of Hulda's brothers* offered us their home in Saskatoon for a month while they ministered in Camps. We enjoyed those weeks alone as a family.

Pete and Anne Schroeder

Hulda's older sister, Mary, was returning from missionary work in South America for furlough on June 11th and it was nice we could meet her.

At this time of the year we were making arrangements to return to Africa.

Back in Herbert again it was time to attend a Bible Camp out on a farm nearby. After that I did some stooking on another farm for two weeks. This was great to be back doing the work that I had done many years ago in Australia.

During September and October of 1952, Hulda's parents and sisters offered to look after our twins while Hulda and I went to Beamsville, Ontario to visit our Canadian mission headquarters. We took our oldest son, Ron, with us and while there, he had to have a hernia operation and was in hospital in Toronto for three days. While staying in Toronto with our friends of the Christian Literature Crusade, we were able to attend a service at the People's Church where Dr. Oswald Smith was the senior pastor.

On our way back to Herbert we stayed over for a few days in Regina to visit another of Hulda's sisters, her husband and their two daughters.* There in Regina, a meeting was arranged for us to speak to the students at the Canadian Bible College, which was a college of the Christian and Missionary Alliance.

* Luella and Ted Epp, Beverley and Brenda

After taking a few more meetings and spending Christmas with the Schroeder family, it was time for us to start moving again. We left Herbert on January 6th, 1953 for our mission headquarters again in Ontario, and then across to our USA headquarters in Philadelphia. We were able to purchase a half-ton truck with money that Hulda's family had generously given to us, and this truck was shipped from New York to Mombasa, East Africa. We were able to make bookings on the RMS Queen Elizabeth and sailed to England. From there we sailed on another ship (through the Mediterranean and down through the Suez Canal to Kenya's port city of) Mombasa, where our truck was waiting for us. We were able to put our baggage and belongings into the truck and started driving inland to our mission field in Congo.

See 'First Furlough Map' in the Map section of the blog.

The trip inland from Mombasa was not without fear. We left late in the afternoon after our baggage was cleared through customs and loaded on to the truck. When evening came we felt we should stop and camp for the night. We found a hotel and had a meal. While we were eating, a white man came in and as he sat down at a table, he placed his gun right on the table. This was something we had not seen before in Kenya.

We had heard quite a lot about the Mau Mau trouble in Kenya. A number of people were praying for our safety, that God would put his guardian angels around us as we travelled by day and as we slept by night. We had a good night's rest and early on Easter Sunday we started off for Nairobi. We had sent word to our friends there and they welcomed us to their home on arrival that evening. They told us to draw the curtains in our bedroom as everything was supposed to be kept dark. They advised us to leave early next day, but not before dawn and told us not to stop anywhere or get out of the truck, until we had passed through the danger area. But alas, we were short on gas. What were we to do? On the outskirts of Nairobi on that Easter Monday there was a service station open so we pulled up and it seemed safe to fill up. The attendant was paid, I got back into the truck and away we went without incident. Truly our God was watching over us.

How relieved we all were when at evening time we had passed out of the danger zone and had arrived at a mission station at Kisumu, where kind missionaries took us in.

The next portion of the trip after leaving Kisumu, was to cross the border from Kenya into Uganda. On from there, we made our way to Namirembe Guest House in Kampala, run by the Church Missionary Society.

What a lovely view we had high up on that hill overlooking Kampala. We could see for miles around with the beautiful Anglican Cathedral right behind us and the mission hospital across the road. It was a haven of rest for these weary travelers.

The next stage of the journey was from Kampala to Fort Portal. Here we could see the Ruwenzori Mountains across the border in Congo. The following day we came to the border between Uganda and Congo. The Belgian official at the customs post asked how long we had owned the truck and how many miles we had driven it and then declared it duty free.

We crossed the border and were now in the Congo. Be alert! You don't drive on the left side of the road any longer, but keep to the right.

As we journeyed on, things became more familiar to us. At night fall, around 6 pm, we tried to find a place to stay in Beni but there was no room available so we got wearily back into the truck. We knew there was no other place to stay for the night until several hours further along the road at Oicha, where there was an Africa Inland Mission station. On we went and upon our arrival, the missionaries there were very hospitable and took us in, even though it was late at night.

Leaving Oicha, where there was a large Leprosy hospital, we drove further west to our own mission station at Ibambi, arriving safely on April 13th. We stayed at Ibambi for a week or so as this was the headquarters of our mission. The field director lived here as well as several other missionaries. Some taught in the Bible School, others were involved in printing material for the Congolese church and others did medical work.

The field director called us into his office one day and asked us to start our next term of service at a station far to the south. The missionaries serving at Opienge were soon due for furlough and he felt that this new assignment for us was of the Lord. We felt the same and made preparations to move down to the station that was about 250 miles to the south. We went first to town* to buy some provisions to take along with us, as Opienge was tucked away in the Ituri forest and far from any stores or other white people. ** I had previously been at Opienge in 1941 and had stayed there two weeks before trekking even further south to another station at Lubutu. My wife had never been there, and for her it meant learning a new language.

* probably Paulis
** Another of Aubrey's simple statements but full of unsaid meaning. Imagine taking a young family into what was essentially the middle of the Ituri rain forest in the early 1950s. The lonely government outpost and mission station were at the end of a little-used secondary road, long hours away from any medical help or stores. While there was help to be had with washing diapers, cooking and cleaning, one still had to find suitable food for the children, keep them under mosquito nets at night, think of schooling, books, toys, vaccinations, all the while being aware of where they are playing so they don't encounter any of the local fauna that crawl and slither - more about that in the next chapter.

Chapter 5

Second Term
1953 to 1959

Ron, Ken, Carol, Aubrey, Hulda and David ready to return to Opienge, 1958

Opienge

1953 to 1959

On arriving at Opienge in April, we had a great welcome from both the missionaries and Congolese. We were happy to work with our senior missionaries, Mr. and Mrs. Ivor Davies. They had their two daughters with them at Opienge.

We were very impressed on our first Sunday as we entered the church to hear such hearty singing with wonderful harmony. Mr. Davies had taught the tonic sol-fa and the congregation of about two hundred could sing four-part harmony.

Mr. Davies asked me to help in the boys' school. The school was small, only fifty boys, but in the girls' school there were seventy students. There were two tribes in this area and the custom was to sell off their daughters long before they were ready for marriage, just to obtain more wealth. This was a pagan custom, and when these people became Christians, they agreed to send their children to school. The reason there were so few boys in school was because there was a local false cult that was opposed to the gospel.

After much prayer and keeping steadily on preaching in the villages, the opposition broke down and we soon had good numbers of boys in our schools. I was then able to open several schools in the villages where there were churches. Many of our future pastors and evangelists grew up in these schools. Young men and women preferred to have a Christian marriage rather than a pagan marriage, and it was my privilege to marry several couples at Opienge.

Another impression of Opienge we had upon arriving was the definite seeking for, and prayer for, revival. The people in this area had received a visit from some visiting preachers from the small country of Ruanda* east of Congo. The Ruanda revival had been going on for some years and these keen preachers were spreading the revival message and blessing over into the Congo. The Opienge church had said "We need what these preachers have."

* now Rwanda

A few weeks after we had arrived at Opienge, news came up from Lubutu, the station south of us, that extraordinary things were happening down there. There was a great conviction of sin among the Christians and after confession of sin there was liberty and great joy among the people. God worked among the pagans as well and many were saved.

A Christian woman came to Opienge from Lubutu and in one of our meetings she began to shake and tremble. Some thought she was sick. It wasn't sickness, but a burden for revival to come among the people at Opienge.

At one meeting I attended, the local pastor's wife asked to speak. She told the congregation of what the Lord had been telling her. She said. "When we want to light a fire in the mornings, what is the first thing we do? Is it not that we take a broom and sweep away the ashes from the fire place where yesterday's fire had gone out? We then place the wood in order and then go and get a live coal from someone else's fire and light the fire and it burns brightly. But if we don't clean the ashes away the fire isn't very good."

Then the woman made the application saying, "We Christians need to clean the ashes out of our hearts and then the fire of God will burn in our hearts."

Immediately there was a moving of God's Spirit in our midst and that was the beginning of revival at Opienge. God did more in a few hours than missionaries had done over years of toil. Many of the church leaders were the first to confess their sins and others followed. Meetings went on for hours at a time. When folks got right with God, there was great liberty.

The congregation would stand and with hands raised toward heaven would sing and praise the Lord Jesus for his precious blood which cleanses from all sin, 1 John 1:9 *If we confess our sins, He is faithful and just to forgive us our sins, and to cleanse us from all unrighteousness. NKJV*

These revival meetings continued on for several months and revival blessing spread out into the area and to other mission stations. The story of this revival in 1953 is recorded in the booklet *This is That.*

This was a 1954 booklet edited by Norman Grubb who was head of WEC at the time. It has long been out of print, and a second edition published in 2000 with an introduction by Dr. Helen Roseveare is also out of print. It was called The Spirit of Revival. A digital version of that booklet can be found via the link in the blog.

Besides being involved in the boys' school where I had a meeting every morning before breakfast and taught in some classes, I visited many of the thirty churches in the area.

Those six and a half years of my missionary career were the most enjoyable of my life. I preached morning and evening and three times on Sundays for weeks at a time. What greater joy could a person have then to lead poor lost souls to the foot of the cross. These Balumbi and Wakumu people responded in great numbers to the gospel.

Hulda was not always able to go out with me to visit the area churches, only when the schools were on holidays. Then we would go out as a family into the villages and preach in the open air and teach the Christians in a church, if they had one. Hulda faithfully stayed by the stuff and kept the home fires burning when I was out. As the children got older, Hulda started school for the three of them following a correspondence course from Canada.

In 1954, the Davies family left for furlough. I took them to Stanleyville where they boarded a plane to return to Britain. We certainly did miss them as we were now alone.

Later on in the year, the field director brought down a senior lady missionary to take over the girls' school. Miss Harman* was a school teacher and also a nurse. We liked her very much and it was nice to have a nurse around when the children got sick. The nearest Doctor was about 90 miles away at Bafwasende, which was three and a half hours drive from where we were living.

* This is the same Miss Harman that had been the nurse at Ronnie's birth at Wamba, and a decade later would be shot by the rebels in Stanleyville.

At both Christmas and Easter, we held conferences on the mission station. The Christians and elders of the thirty district churches would come and spend a few days together. The Word was preached, believers examined and baptized. What happy times these were! The Christians wouldn't come empty handed. Those who could afford would bring a chicken or some eggs for the missionaries and their families.

In January of 1955, the church decided to evangelize six villages in a remote corner of our area. Some of the evangelists were a bit afraid to go as there were rumors that much witchcraft was carried on amongst these people. The church asked me if I would be willing to make the long trek over to these people and I felt I should go. If I went, then some of the Congolese were also keen about going.

We all went as a family in our truck for seventy-five miles to our last out-church at Bilota. Miss Harman came along with us.

The journey would mean many hours of walking through dense jungle, so the ladies and children stayed at the church in Bilota, and I set off with a team of pastors and evangelists to survey the situation and see if anything further could be done for these people. It was a long walk. The first day we walked five hours and camped the night in the forest by a stream of water. The next day we walked another four and a half hours and camped again. On the third day, we arrived at the first of the six villages, all soaking wet as the rain caught us before we got to the village. We had walked some forty miles over a muddy, rough path.

We spent two days with the people of the first village and they received us well and without too much opposition. Then we went on to the second village, about twelve miles further along. These villages were far apart. The people were poor and suffering with no medical service to help them. The third village was another ten-mile walk. Here I stopped as my legs were aching. The teachers went on and taught the people in the next three villages, then returned to where I had been resting up for the return journey. I had eight porters carrying my camp cot, food box and baggage. Some of the school boys and school girls from Bilota came along with us for the fun of travelling with a white man. Altogether we were thirty-two in the party. No missionary had ever been to this isolated part of

Congo where about 250 people lived who needed to hear the gospel. During our stay with them, fourteen made a decision to follow Christ.

We left one teacher to work with them after we returned to Bilota. The return trip took only two days; the last day we walked from early morning to evening. What a day! Was I ever tired, but it was nice to be back again with the family. Ron, our oldest son who was five years of age then, had learned to ride his mother's bicycle while I was away those two weeks.

After a day's rest we packed our things into the truck and visited one more out-church and taught there, then returned to Opienge.

The next month in February our three children came down with measles. When one was just about over it, the next would get sick.

Hulda had planned a women's conference for the end of February and was delighted to see 200 women attend.

At the end of October, Ron had his 6th birthday and the twins Carol and Ken celebrated their 4th birthday in December. Hulda had made two cakes for them.

A Greek trader had his birthday the day before the twins and for his birthday he had killed a pig, so he shared some of the pork for the birthday party at our house. This coffee plantation owner was kind and helped us often by bringing back supplies from Kisangani whenever he took a load of coffee to market. He also owned several native shops.

There were sometimes scorpions in the leaves that made up the thatch roof of our house. Sometimes they would appear on the walls. One day Carol put her hand in a mortar to take something and didn't see the scorpion there. It stung her and she cried with pain for the longest time.

Early in the year of 1956, we received a letter from our field director, Mr. Scholes. He said that he and his wife were planning a visit to Opienge, and they would be accompanied by our mission doctor so she could see the work at Opienge. Her name was Dr. Helen Roseveare.

Opienge was a small Government Post, and as it was at the end of the road, it got lonely at times. We felt cut off from our other missionaries, so visitors were always welcome. We, as well as the Congolese, enjoyed their visit so much that one of our children cried when it came time for our visitors to return to Ibambi.

In March, we planned our yearly shopping trip to Stanleyville as we needed to stock up again on provisions for another year. This trip took eight hours in our truck. We stayed overnight and returned the next day. The children enjoyed these trips to the big city to see what civilization was like. It was a long way to go, hot and tiring, and we were exhausted by the time we got back home.

In July, Mr. Scholes, asked me if I would take a missionary family to Rhino Camp in Uganda. They had three small children and were due for furlough. Rhino Camp is a port on the Nile River where the river steamer stopped to pick up passengers.

This trip took two weeks. The Lord helped us and we had no trouble. We stayed overnight at different mission stations where folks were so hospitable and kind. When we arrived at the Nile, the steamer was there. We said goodbye, and I started my long journey home. This family moved up the river, crossed some lakes and then caught a train down to the coast of Kenya. There they got on board a ship to England.

This was the identical journey to the African coast taken by Aubrey, Hulda, and Ronnie several years earlier as they left on their first furlough.

The area around Opienge was dense forest. The people were easy to reach because the Belgian government had arranged for the people to come out of the forest and to live in villages on the motor roads. From Opienge, we had three main roads where we could go with our truck and visit the thirty churches and other villages where no church as yet had come into being.

In 1957, Hulda organized eight conferences for women. They would be held in central places along these three roads instead of all the women coming on to the mission station. It proved a success and more women were reached with the gospel.

In about six months, we were expecting our fourth child. Hulda needed to get away for a rest and change, so I took her and Ron over to our friends who were on another mission station amongst a different tribe. I returned with the twins to Opienge. One day one of the children came quickly back from the outside toilet and said a green snake was there. I got hold of a spear and went outside and soon killed it before it had time to escape.

There were two kinds of snakes in the area. One was the black mamba which was five to six feet long. The other was a thin green snake about two to three feet long. Both were dangerous. As folks were praying for our safety, the Lord protected us from being bitten by snakes.

We left Opienge at 6:30 am on December 20th to go to the hospital at Nebobongo to have our fourth child. We intended to drive as far as Bafwapoko where there was a place to stay overnight. We hadn't gone far when we came to a stop. A fair-sized tree had blown down across the road and there was no way to pass. We had to wait three hours until the tree was cut away by nearby villagers and then we could drive on.

Further along, we had to stop again. This time a small bridge had broken and again we waited an hour before it was fixed and we could cross over. Delays are not uncommon in Africa and it was hard for Hulda as we were on the road for ten and a half hours.

Hulda was by this time, three weeks away from having her fourth child.

From Bafwapoko, we drove to Wamba the following day. Here we stayed over the weekend and I was asked to preach Sunday morning to the 350 people who came to worship.

On Monday we drove on to Ibambi where we stayed for ten days, which included Christmas. The Christians from many out-churches in the district gathered at Ibambi for the Christmas conference and Mr. Scholes asked me to speak on Christmas morning. What a crowd! There were 2000 in the large brick church and about as many sitting outside under temporary palm-frond lean-tos around the windows of the church. The group of about one thousand children that had come with their parents had separate meetings in the school. It was reported that five thousand people came to that conference. When I spoke that morning, they used loud speakers for the crowd to hear. I spoke in the Kiswahili language and it was then interpreted into three tribal languages. That takes a long time. I said two or three sentences; one man would interpret into Kibudu, the second man into Kiluka, and the third into Kiyogo. I didn't understand nor could I speak any of these three tribal languages. A half-hour message then, would take around two hours to reach everybody's ears. The second meeting that day went from 10:30 am until 3:30 pm. By that time, I was getting a headache and it was very hot with so many people packed in the church. However, God worked and souls were saved.

In the new year of 1958, we moved to the hospital station nearby called Nebobongo to await our baby. It was decided that I would take Ron and Ken and stay at Deti. There was an out-church and a rest house there for us to live in. I taught in the early morning meetings and after breakfast I did school with Ron and Ken. Deti was situated on a high hill from which we had a wonderful view over the forest and grassland. Carol was invited to another station where there was another girl her age with whom she would be able to play.

On January 12, just before midnight, David Henry Brown was born. The next morning a Congolese came to Deti on a bicycle to tell us the news that Ron and Ken had a baby brother. What excitement it was for all of us! We put away the school books and declared a holiday. We packed up our camp cots and loaded up the truck. We took the messenger, Luka, with his bike, and headed for Nebobongo. After an hour's drive we arrived and soon were admiring the new baby and talking with Hulda.

After a couple of weeks or so it was time to move back south to our work at Opienge. We arrived home on February 4 and it was time to start the schools. Schools for men, women, boys, girls - and missionary kids.

It was early 1958, and we had now been at Opienge for five years. Hulda had taught our three older children to read, so now they could spend many a happy hour reading their story books.

As the rains had come in March, Hulda enjoyed planting dahlias and roses. Bushes of bougainvillea, gardenias and honeysuckles helped to brighten things up around our home. There were lots of tall palm trees around our house also.

The month of May was when taxes were collected and every Congolese man had to pay tax. Those fathers who had four children had to pay much less than the others. Missionaries were exempt from paying taxes on vehicles and bicycles; we were taxed on radios only.

Ron could now read well but he had no Bible, so as I had inherited my Grandpa Brown's Bible, I wrote home to my sister and asked her to send it out to us. It came in due time and Ron began reading a portion of it every day. Ken and Carol had an old New Testament of ours, which they read each day.

One day, two Belgian ladies brought gifts of clothing for our new baby.

In August, we arranged a conference for Christians in the area and sent invitations out to all our mission stations to send a delegation of pastors, evangelists and some believers. We stipulated the number as we could not handle too many. Eleven missionaries were able to come and one hundred and fifty Congolese, counting our Opienge folk. What a blessed week of meetings we had. We heard good teaching from visiting pastors; there were times of sharing, good singing and praise to the Lord. The Opienge church did a good job in providing food and lodging for their visitors. They also brought food for us and the visiting missionaries.

Later in the year, Miss Winnie Davies, our nurse and fellow worker, wanted to buy a vehicle to get around in. We arranged a trip to Stanleyville to see what we could find. Ron came along with us. Winnie chose an Opel Caravan and after we finished purchasing the car, and then finished our shopping, we set out on the eight-hour journey for home. Winnie drove the Opel and we followed in our truck.

Four years later, Winnie Davies was taken from Opienge in late 1964 by a rebel unit and held for thirty-four months before being killed.

Several visits were made into the area where we preached and taught. Our district schools were also visited and another conference at Christmas. In all 1958 was a good year. We experienced the Lord's help and blessing, His protection and provision.

Early in 1959, our family went out for a three-week trek. We set a goal to preach and teach in every village along a certain road. We thought perhaps this would be our last time along these roads as furlough was coming up in the future. I would leave Hulda and the four children where there was a suitable rest house near to a church. Then I would stay in villages on either side of where the rest of the family was staying. When we finished one section we would move to another section along the road. We averaged preaching in two villages each day. Hulda was able to take meetings where she stayed and I preached in the villages, morning and evening.

After we had preached in these fourteen villages, we returned to the mission station to attend to things waiting for us. Soon it was time to reach villages along the Wande Road. Ken accompanied me for two weeks and we visited and taught in all the villages along this road; four souls made profession of faith in Christ during these meetings.

On the station at Opienge, there were three couples among our teachers who were ready to obey the Lord's call to leave home and loved ones, and take the glorious message of the gospel to tribes further south who were still in heathen darkness.

In June, I drove up to Ibambi for field committee meetings and this time I took Ron along. Our furlough was discussed at one of these meetings, and so letters were sent from the field director to the Home Base leaders at London Headquarters to start making arrangements.

In July, Hulda and Carol went along with Winnie Davies to do some shopping in Stanleyville. I stayed home with the three boys. A few weeks later, I had to go to Stanleyville to buy iron roofing for the maternity building which we were erecting at Opienge. Our return trip took thirteen hours as twice we found trucks stuck in the mud and we could not pass until they moved.

News at the MK school at this time was that Ron was doing grade 5 and the twins were doing grade 3.

The field director wrote a letter to us and asked us to go ahead and try to make a booking on a ship going from Mombasa to England. We did this and received a favorable reply. There was a ship due in Mombasa on December 15th and heading for England. We then contacted someone who was interested in buying our truck and with that money and personal gifts, we were able to pay for our passage and sail from Mombasa, East Africa.

The Church leaders at Opienge were happy to hear that we were making arrangements to leave. There was much unrest in Congo at this time as the people wanted their independence from Belgium*. One could feel the anti-white sentiment around us. When we were all packed up and ready to leave, the church leaders presented us with a gift of money of over one hundred dollars. It was a love gift from them that they had given to us out of their poverty. They said, "Your children will need clothing along the way." This really touched our hearts.

This was the start of the independence turmoil that lasted from mid-1960 until late in 1965. Many countries in Africa were getting out from under colonial rule and Congo also wanted to be free from the Belgians' rule. There was tension all over the country and Aubrey and his family avoided a lot of trouble by leaving at this time. At Opienge, there were obviously some mixed feelings involved as on the one hand, the church leaders wanted to have full responsibility for decision-making and the direction of the church and its growth, but on the other hand, they were sorry to see the family go, as there seemed to be mutual love and respect all around.

We said goodbye to our Opienge friends and to the government officials at the post office, and drove to Wamba where we left our truck.

The field director had arranged for fellow missionary Frank Bates to take us and our baggage in the mission truck to Kasese in Uganda. This was the railway terminal in western Uganda, and when we arrived there, we met a party of our own missionaries returning from their furlough in England. Mr Bates was able to put their baggage on the truck and take them back to Congo. We boarded the train and after passing through Kampala and Nairobi, we arrived at Kenya's port city of Mombasa.

Our boat arrived a day or so after we did. We embarked and were soon on our way home, sailing north up the eastern coast of Africa. We celebrated Christmas while sailing through the Red Sea and approaching the Suez Canal. The children were invited to a party in the first-class lounge. They enjoyed the Christmas tree and the gifts they received from the crew. There were lots of new things for these children to see having just come from deep in the forest of Congo.

When we arrived in London, my friend, Fred Anthony, a staff member of the mission, accompanied by a new mission candidate, met us at the docks with two cars and soon we were at London WEC headquarters. The weather was extremely cold and most of us got sick. There was sad news awaiting us when we arrived in London; Hulda's father was very ill. We only stayed four days in London. On the morning we were to leave, Ronnie fell ill. Our bookings were made to leave from Liverpool that day and we soon had to catch the train from London to Liverpool. What were we to do?* Our only resort was to pray and anoint Ronnie with oil and believe God for this healing. We did this. When we got off the train at Liverpool, Ronnie was so weak that he couldn't stand up and so he went over and sat against a wall while we were arranging for a taxi to take us down to the boat. His mother said to him, "Ronnie I know you are feeling very sick, but try and not look sick until we get on the ship!" He was a brave boy and we all made it on to the boat. When we found our cabin, the children were able to go to bed.

* The concern was that they wouldn't be allowed on the ship with a sick child as a contagious illness could spread throughout the ship, but they couldn't afford to wait for the next ship crossing the Atlantic due to the deteriorating health of Hulda's father.

It took us six days to cross the Atlantic and arrive in Halifax, Nova Scotia. From there we got on a train and after three days and three nights on the train, we arrived safely in Swift Current, Saskatchewan where Hulda's parents had just moved into a new house. There were several of Hulda's family there to meet us at the train station and others came later in the evening to see us. Being away seven years from the family, it was so good to see them all again.

It was January 24, and we gave thanks to God for watching over us on our long seven and a half week journey from Opienge to Swift Current.

Chapter 6

Second Furlough
1960 to 1962

FAMILY PORTRAIT, 1962

Canada and Australia

1960 to 1962

After arriving in Swift Current, Saskatchewan on January 24, we spent a week with Hulda's folks, then moved to Herbert and into the house where her parents had lived previously. It was near the local school and our children were enrolled there. We didn't have a car, so Hulda's sister Emma, let us use her car for a whole year while we were on furlough. This was a sacrifice for her. Hulda's brother bought overshoes and caps for our children so that they could play outside in the snow. We found the weather very cold.

Three of the local churches had grocery showers for us. This was a great help to us in setting up our home in Herbert and we were so thankful for their love and generosity.

After we had been in Canada for five weeks, we received a phone call from Swift Current to say that Hulda's father, Mr. Isaac Schroeder, had passed away. It was March 2. Our family attended the funeral together with the other members of the large Schroeder family.

March 21 marked the first day of spring; the days were getting warmer and the snow was melting away. Over the last two months, our children had been learning to skate on the ice.

From time to time I was able to help on the Schroeder family farm. It was near Main Centre, a short drive from Herbert, and was where Hulda was born and grew up. She lived there until she left for Bible School, and then later left for missionary work in Africa where I met her. I enjoyed driving the tractor and being out on the land again.

Before I knew it, the time had come to begin travelling and speaking at meetings in the churches, Bible Schools and missionary conferences. These meetings took me around Saskatchewan and other provinces. I was able to show missionary films and distribute literature relating to the needs of various mission fields.

Later on, in 1960 we received a letter asking us if we would be interested in pastoring a church in north-western Saskatchewan for a while. We considered this, as we could be all together instead of my being on the road so much away from the family. We drove up to this place to see it and met with the leader of the church council. The man we wanted to see was out in the field harvesting so we drove out there for a short interview. We decided to accept the position and so we left Herbert and moved to the small farming community of Lashburn around September when the schools started again for another year. We lived in the parsonage right next to the church. Now I had to study and prepare sermons as I had to preach at two services on Sunday, a weekly Bible study and prayer meeting, as well as visitation to do.

At Christmas time we were able to arrange to be with the Schroeder family in Swift Current. Then after Christmas, as our year was nearly up in Canada, we started making plans to go to Australia to see my folks before returning to Africa for another term

We went back to Lashburn for a few weeks and arranged for our leaving. Then we returned to Herbert, said goodbye to our relatives and friends, and then took our flight to Vancouver.

From there, we flew over the Pacific Ocean to Sydney, Australia with a short stop-over in Hawaii.*

What a difference a decade makes. On the last furlough in 1952, it took the family nineteen days to cross the Pacific in an ocean liner, whereas at this point in the story, 1961, an airliner made the crossing in just over a day. In 2019 that journey is now 15 and a half hours.

Our WEC mission folks were at the Sydney airport to meet us and take us to the headquarters in Strathfield, one of the suburbs. After a brief stay there, we took the train south to Victoria. At Albury, on the border between New South Wales and Victoria, we were met by my brother Rupert and his wife

Evelyn in one car, and my uncle Charlie Wood and Auntie Ida in their car. They drove us all the way to Bendigo, which was a long drive. We arrived in the evening and were met by my mother and sister who were waiting for us.

I enjoyed staying at home for several weeks and catching up on the news of relatives and friends. Rupert, Evelyn and their son Rodney lived close by and we saw them often. We spoke at a few meetings arranged for us.

One day we received a message from a farmer near Bridgewater, a town about twenty miles northwest of Bendigo. He asked if we would be interested in living in one of the two houses on his farm. We went out to see the place which was available, and talked with the Christian friends who owned the farm. We felt this was God's provision for us and so we moved out to this country home. For the first time, our children went to school by bus. We enjoyed the farm with the purebred Border Leicester sheep grazing around our house and in the wide-open fields. The land produced good crops of wheat.

Rupert gave us the use of his car to get around in during our furlough and so we were able to attend the local church and Sunday School as well as get back and forth to Bendigo.

The mission assigned me to deputation meetings* in the states of Queensland, South Australia and Western Australia while Hulda stayed with the children in Bridgewater. At one point I was asked to fill in at the WEC National Headquarters in Sydney while the Australian Director attended an international conference of the mission in Britain. For two weeks I gave messages to the staff and candidates at the HQ.

* When missionaries returned home for a break from their foreign field of service, the mission would assign them meetings, usually in churches, to not only let people know about that individual's work, but also inform them about the mission society and its work, and about missions in general. This brought in new recruits and fostered the relationship between the churches and the mission society, between the financial benefactors and the organization that funneled the money to the missionaries and their work.

In between tours, I was happy to help on the farm driving the tractor. During shearing time, I picked up wool, sorted and put the fleeces in bales. I helped at harvest time driving a truck and hauling grain to the silo or elevator in Bridgewater. The year ended with Christmas, with loved ones and the great convention at Belgrave Heights east of Melbourne which I was able to attend.

The first few months of 1962 were taken up with tours, meetings and helping on the farm.

We were praying and seeking guidance about returning to Africa. We wrote a letter to the principal of Rethy Academy, a school for missionaries' children in Congo operated by the Africa Inland Mission, inquiring if there was a possibility of our children enrolling there. They replied favorably and sent application forms. These were filled in and sent back and an answer came back in due time informing us that they were accepted and that school started in early September.

Our plans were now in motion. The mission inquired about bookings and visas. Congo had no embassy in Australia at that time so our passports had to be sent to Britain to have visas stamped into them.

We received a phone call from the secretary of our mission telling us about a ship departing from Melbourne on a certain date and did we want to book our passage on that ship? By faith I said "Go ahead and make the bookings." We didn't have enough money yet to pay for it, nor did we have our passports back from England. However, we trusted the Lord to work for us.

Rupert and Evelyn arranged a farewell for us in their home on July 23. Then the following day, after saying goodbye to my mother and sister, we left Bendigo and headed for Melbourne. That same night, a farewell had been arranged for us in the People's Church. When we entered the church and had sat down, a lady came and sat behind us and touched Hulda on the shoulder. She passed her an envelope. When we got back to the place we were staying that night, we opened the envelope. Here was an answer to our prayers as we found a fairly large gift of money and that, together with a few other gifts we had received we enough to pay our passage back to the Congo. We had a good farewell in Melbourne.

We still, however, hadn't received our passports back from England and were due to sail the next day from Melbourne. We checked with the captain and he said we could embark on the *Strathcona* without passports and sail as far as Freemantle, in West Australia. If the passports were not there, then we would have to get off the ship. So, the mission con-

tacted London and told them to send our passports to Freemantle instead of Melbourne.

Off we went. It was another opportunity to see God perform a miracle in the next few days.

Faith, mighty faith, the promise sees and looks to God alone;
laughs at impossibilities and cries ,"It shall be done."
Charles Wesley

I was a bad sailor and got sea sick crossing the Australian
Bight. The sea was rough.

At 8 pm our ship docked in Fremantle. What was the first
thing we did on arrival? We went to the purser and asked if
there was any mail for us. Sure enough, he found a large envelope addressed to Aubrey Brown, and that contained our
passports with the necessary visas stamped inside. Our hearts
rejoiced and we gave thanks to God.

A number of our friends came to the boat to see us which
was nice. As we had a five-hour stop, our mission representative came and took us to the WEC headquarters in nearby
Perth, and then on a tour of that beautiful city. He also interviewed us and our conversation was recorded on tape which
was later broadcast on the radio station at Geraldton. Back on
the ship we packed away our winter clothes as the climate was
now much warmer.

Leaving Australia from Freemantle, we set sail for Colombo, arriving on August 7 and two days later we arrived in
Bombay. Our children enjoyed the ship's swimming pool as
they had learnt to swim in Bridgewater; David learned to
swim on the boat at four and a half years.

In Bombay, we had to change to another ship bound for
Mombasa in East Africa. It was leaving in a few days so while
we waited, we stayed at the Red Shield of the Salvation Army.
It was monsoon season in this part of India, and it rained day
after day.

One evening, we went out to hear Bakht Singh* preach as
he was holding meetings in Bombay. Another day, two of
Hulda's friends who were missionaries at the Mukti Mission**
came to Bombay to see us. They hired a taxi and showed us
around the city of Bombay which was so interesting.

* Baght Singh was India's foremost evangelist and a pioneer of indigenous church-planting.
**Mukti Mission was dedicated to helping and educating women and girls in the slums of Bombay (now Mumbai).

When we left Bombay, we had one stopover in the Seychelles* before we arrived in Mombasa. We passed through customs, and in the evening left by train for Nairobi arriving there at 8 am the next day.

* The Seychelles are a group of islands off the east coast of Africa, lying north of both the large island of Madagascar and the smaller islands of the Comoros. The latter was where Aubrey's son Ken, with Teresa and family spent a term working with Africa Inland Mission.

In Nairobi we shopped around for a vehicle and soon found a 1959 Opel Station Wagon which registered 30,000 miles.* Whether that was the true mileage or not we did not know, but we bought it and set off for Congo. The first day we drove 450 miles from Nairobi to Kampala, Uganda arriving at 10 pm. From Kampala, we drove west to Kasese where the railway line ended and where we could pick up our baggage that had been shipped by train from Mombasa. Here our mission truck was waiting to meet us and our baggage was loaded onto that truck as well as some other missionaries that had arrived there. That night we slept in the vehicles, some in the car and some in the truck, as the hotel there was too expensive for us.

* In Hulda's book, "River of Memories", she mentions that her sister, Emma, had called her in Australia the morning of the day they set sail from Melbourne. She asked if they had enough money for the trip and Hulda said they had enough to get to Africa but not enough yet for a vehicle to drive inland. Emma asked where to send money for that, and Aubrey told her to send funds to the Bank of Nairobi. Thus, with the Schroeder family's generosity, and some money that Aubrey's mother had given them for a car, they had enough to purchase the used car in Nairobi. The Opel car was similar to the one Winnie Davies had found in Kisangani, mentioned in the previous chapter.

The next day we left Kasese and headed for the Congo border. The Congolese officials at Customs let our baggage go through without charging anything, but they refused to let us enter Congo. They said our passports were not in order. We turned back and stayed in a government rest house on Lake Edward for the night, where we saw lots of hippos. In the morning we drove south a few hundred miles to a different Customs post and there the Lord undertook for us and the official gave us visitor's visas to enter Congo. We drove across the border a short way and then pulled over to the side of the road and had a little prayer meeting. We gave thanks to God for His help on our behalf.

From the border we drove to Rethy where we left our three older children. Rethy Academy was a school for missionary children and they had about sixty students. We said goodbye to our children and headed for Ibambi mission station, averaging twenty-five miles per hour as the roads were in bad condition. We arrived safely at 9 pm on September 7.

There we were told by the missionaries that the truck carrying our baggage had broken down in the middle of the forest. A few days later I went with Bill McChesney, a new American missionary and mechanic, in a pick-up truck back to where our baggage was in the broken-down truck. We removed the broken engine out of the larger truck and put it in the back of the pick-up truck. Then we removed the engine from the pick-up truck and put that one in the larger mission truck. Then we towed the pick-up truck behind the larger truck and returned to Ibambi. That was a huge job.* We were thankful that none of our things were stolen, mainly because a faithful Congolese worker had been watching over our things there in the forest.

* A vehicle engine swap by the side of the road in the middle of a remote jungle with limited tools and facilities - yes, that would have been quite a job! They would have had to cut down several trees to make a sturdy framework on which to hang a block and tackle with chains to lift the engines in and out. But from what I've heard and read, that is what made Bill McChesney so special, not only a great mechanic but one who could improvise - a necessity in the middle of Africa. Neither Aubrey or Bill could have known that in less than two years, the Simbas would murder this talented young man.

Chapter 7

Third Term
1962 to 1964

THE BROWN FAMILY'S PRAYER CARD, CIRCA 1962

Poko

1962 to 1964

After the repair to the mission truck, enabling our baggage to arrive in Ibambi, we spent a few days with the missionaries there. One day the field director, Jack Scholes, called us over to his house and asked us to go to Poko station in the northwest for our third term in the Congo.

We arrived in Poko on September 26. The station had been left two years without resident missionaries and we found the house dirty and the roof leaking where we were supposed to live. The Congolese Christians welcomed us and quickly mended the roof on our house.

We noticed several differences between the Poko area and Opienge, where we had spent our last term. Instead of forest and jungle it was grassland with not as many trees. People were harder to reach with the gospel as they were so scattered, not living together in villages. Hulda and I had to switch from using Swahili, to speaking in the Bangala language which we used during our first term at Nala many years ago. The soil on the station was a dark red and David's clothes didn't stay clean very long when he was out playing with the Congolese children. Also, we found the climate hotter than down south at Opienge.

In Poko, we collected our mail at the Government Post and were happy to receive the first letters from Rethy where our older children were doing school. Besides the Post, there was a hospital, a few Greek traders running several shops, and some Belgians on nearby coffee plantations. We noticed that the country had deteriorated since its independence in July 1960, when many Belgians had left the country.

In December, I went back to Rethy to pick up the three children and bring them home for the Christmas holidays. It took a week for the round trip.

Dr. Roseveare lent us her ¼-ton truck to go to Opienge to pick up our belongings stored there. Ron and a Congolese driver came with me. We left at five in the morning and arrived at Opienge at 10:30 pm. What a day! It was good to see the Opienge folk again and they asked me to speak at the Sunday morning service. We loaded our things on to the truck. Our Congolese helper, who worked for us at Opienge, agreed to come and work for us again at our new posting. There was room for him and his wife and four children. We certainly appreciated Dawidi for his faithful service in our home and for his willingness to come and help us again.

Soon it was time to make preparations for the Christmas conference when a thousand or so people came to Poko station from the surrounding churches to celebrate the Saviour's birth. They would stay for about three days, bringing their sleeping mats and food with them. Often, they would bring some food for us as well, such as chickens, eggs and bananas. On Christmas Day we had five meetings. Souls were saved and twenty-two believers were baptized. On Boxing Day, the custom was for the missionaries to eat the evening meal outside with them, which we did.

The new year of 1963, saw us focusing on the larger Poko area for which we were responsible to preach the gospel and build up the existing churches which numbered about eighty. It was quite a task, and involved a lot of travel as the churches were spread out over a wide area. This area consisted of three different tribes: Azande, Barambo, and Amadi but most of the people understood the trade language which we knew and used, Bangala.

We visited many of the eighty churches in our area and when we were back on the mission station, I was teaching students to upgrade their knowledge of the Bible. Some of the students would then go on to Bible School, others would return to their village and work with the pastor or start another church.

Three times a year I made the three-day long trip to Rethy to get our children from school and after the holidays drive the three-days to take them back again. This meant six long trips in a year. One time I remember Hulda, David and I drove to Rethy and picked up the other three children, then we went on, crossed into Uganda and drove to Kampala. We stayed at the Namirembe Guest House overlooking Kampala and the impressive Anglican Cathedral on the hill nearby. The congregation who worshipped in the Cathedral was evangelical believers as the revival movement had spread widely over countries in eastern Africa.

We did some business and shopping in Kampala, stocking up on supplies we couldn't get in Paulis, and then drove back to Rethy. We stayed there a few days with the children until school started, then returned to Poko.

Sometimes our fellow missionaries would purchase provisions such as gas, kerosene, flour and milk cheaper than we could in our area, and would drop them off at Poko as they were passing through.

Again, at the end of the year there was the Christmas conference held at Poko, where God moved in hearts and lives.

During the latter part of 1963 and early 1964, one could sense an undercurrent of unrest among the people of Congo. There was talk of revolution.

Early in the new year, we had a surprise visit from a missionary whom we knew and who was working among the pygmies. I had mentioned to him at one time, when on one of our trips to Rethy, that I was interested in buying his Chevrolet Carryall when he left for furlough. This missionary's wife was in failing health and the doctor's orders were that both of them should return to Britain. On one trip back from Rethy, we called in to see them and they asked us if we were interested in buying some bulk food stores they had from a recent shopping trip in Kampala. We accepted the offer as it helped us and them. We didn't know at the time why we bought all this food, but the Lord knew what was ahead of us.

We also made the deal about the Chevrolet. On their way out of the country, they would drive it to Kampala and leave it there and then on our next trip to Rethy, we would drive on to

Kampala and get it. It so happened that another new truck was coming out from the United States for one of our missionaries, so I needed to arrange two extra drivers to bring these vehicles across the border into Congo from Uganda.

Just before Easter, Hulda and I set off on the four-day trip to Kampala with two other WEC missionaries. In Kampala, we found the Chev Carryall in good order which I would drive back, one of our missionaries would drive the new Chevrolet truck and the other missionary would take our Opel. After all our business and shopping were done, we left Kampala near evening, and camped by the side of the road for the night. The next day we crossed into Congo and drove to Rethy to pick up our children from school, then headed home to Poko, stopping one more night at Lolwa mission station.

From July 8-15, we attended a field conference of all our missionaries at Ibambi station, then two days later I left for Rethy again. I went first all the way to Kamplala to pick up Florence Stebbing, a missionary who was returning to Congo from England after her furlough. Then we went back to the school to pick up the three children for their second school holiday of the year.

On our journey home, we came around a bend in the road and were met with what looked like a group of soldiers who were marching along with sticks on their shoulders instead of rifles. We didn't exactly know what was going on, but we arrived safely back at Poko on July 27.

THE LAST FAMILY PICTURE BEFORE THE REBELS TAKE OVER - MALINGWIA, 1964

Rebels, Prison and Rescue

July to December, 1964

The previous chapter ended just prior to the rebels moving into the Poko area. So chronologically, this chapter should tell the story of Aubrey's time in rebel-controlled territory, his imprisonment, and the rescue by mercenaries. But the next entry in the typed copy of his manuscript that Ron and I were working with, details the return trip to Canada after the family was safe in Kinshasa. There was nothing about the captivity period. When I went back to the handwritten manuscript, I saw a scrap of paper attached with a paper clip saying that for the rescue story, we should just use the Prayer Letter from January 1965 that covered the facts regarding the rebel period. After re-telling this story over and over again in meetings during the years following the evacuation, it seemed Aubrey had little interest in writing about, and thus re-living those events over twenty-five years later. So what follows is that letter to family, friends and supporters written about a month after returning to Canada. As per Aubrey's style it is bare-bones facts, with little evidence of how he felt or what he was going through.

There is, of course, much more to the story than the facts in that 1965 newsletter. Stories about conflict of this nature are often bereft of detail, as some details are too gruesome to relate and after many years, writing about them takes a toll on the author. Aubrey and his family were spared their lives when others were not, and a brief perusal of some of the articles in the link at the bottom of this post will give you an idea of what other missionaries went through - those that lived and those that didn't. It is not light reading.

247 Central Ave. S.
Swift Current, Sask.
Canada.

January 8, 1965
Dear Praying Friends:

We greet you with Psalm 46:1.* We first want to thank you each one who laboured in prayer for us during these recent four months. God has answered your prayers. If you had not prayed, we may not be here today. I will write this in diary form. You can magnify the Lord with us as you read these facts.
* *God is our refuge and strength, a very present help in trouble.*

July 8 to 15
All of the WEC missionaries along with Congolese delegates met in Conference at Ibambi.

July 17
Left for Rethy to fetch the children from school. Travelled with Dr. Roseveare as far as Nyankunde.

July 23
Brought in Miss Stebbing* from Kampala to Rethy.
* *WEC missionary Florence Stebbing was returning from furlough and bound for the hospital at Nebobongo.*

July 24
Started homeward journey with children.

July 27
Arrived safely home at Poko.

August 6
Tried to go to Paulis but met barriers across the road so had to return. This was the first we knew something was wrong, but we couldn't find out what it was all about.

August 15
Ken and I went seventy miles west to a regional conference. We met up with soldiers of the National Army fleeing from the rebels.* We had a good conference and twenty-one souls were dealt with and five baptized. We took a risk on this trip but the Lord protected us. This was the last time we drove our car. We then hid it in the forest near our station.

When the rebels first started out, they wore bits of animal skins and feathers and used witch doctors at the front of their columns or raids to make up for a lack of modern weapons. The threat of sorcery or spells was too much for many of the National Army and they would often retreat from battles, even though they vastly out-numbered the rebels.

August 25
Poko fell to the rebels after half an hour of shooting. It was a surprise attack and it was only later that we realized another government was taking over. Local Congolese government officials were arrested and beaten; some were shot. We were less than a mile from the Government Post of Poko, so we could hear the shooting. Immediately recruiting began and many young men and boys joined the Popular Army. Good pay and adventure enticed many who had no idea what is was all about.

August 29
Two boys brought us a piece of meat saying it was a gift from the Popular Army. Formerly we bought our meat from the State at a high price. Slowly it dawned upon us that we were now in Communist hands. Barriers were put up on all the roads. Communications were cut off. There was no way out, no mail, no communications with our other mission stations.

September 13
Another two boys about fourteen years of age came with a driver and demanded our car. They pointed a gun at me and said I must hand over the car keys. All local cars and trucks were confiscated by the rebel army. New recruits were called "Jeunesse" (Youth Movement) and after their initiation ceremonies they were made soldiers of the rebel army and called Lions or 'Simbas' in the Swahili language. A new captain came to Poko to take control of the rebels. He was friendly and we learned that he had attended our mission school at Wamba. It

was evident that he was forced into the rebel army (like crowds of others). This captain said he didn't want to kill people. We believe that it was because of him we were let off lightly. God surely arranged this. In other places they were so brutal. The captain with six or eight other Simbas used to attend our Sunday services. One rebel got right with God and other rebels came and bought Bibles. We gave them tracts* and talked with them about the Lord.

Not a common word anymore, but the meaning relevant here, is that of a small pamphlet meant to persuade someone in a political or religious way.

October 20
Poko had a visit from Christophe Gbenye*, the rebel leader from Stanleyville. He told us he had taken Lumumba's place. He denounced civilization and Missions. One soon knew he was a very wicked man. His speech was terrible and frightening. He told the people that Lumumba was their saviour and they should pray to him in trouble.

November 4
Up to this time we carried on with all our meetings. They told us when they came that we could carry on with our meetings until the end of the year. After that they intended to set up their government and then there would be no more Protestant or Catholic religion, but they would set up their communist regime and would put their school teachers into our schools.

November 4
I was arrested and taken to prison where I found twelve other Belgians and one Dutchman. We had four guards. The prison had a corrugated iron roof and the heat from 10 am until 4 pm was almost unbearable. The four guards were on duty twenty-four hours, then changed. Some of them were decent but most of them insulted us and kept threatening to kill us. Hulda was allowed to send food to me which I shared with the others. No reason was given for my arrest. We were told we were prisoners of war.

November 8
Sunday - they allowed me to return to the Mission for the morning service. Then the guard, with a spear, followed me

back to the prison. The Lord gave me a word Monday morning from Psalm 44:5-8. *Through You we will push down our enemies; through Your name we will trample down those who rise up against us. For I will not trust in my bow, nor shall my sword save me. But You have saved us from our enemies and have put to shame those who hated us. In God we boast all day long, and praise Your name forever.*

November 9
Monday evening, I was released. No reason was given. I was told to stay in the house and guards came almost every day to see if I was obeying their orders. During November, Hulda had to cook for the thirteen prisoners.

November 24
Paratroopers came down on Stanleyville. Feeling against all whites began to be very tense.
Aubrey would have heard this on his small short-wave radio but wouldn't have known that it was a major international military operation code-named Operation Dragon Rouge where 350 Belgian paratroopers dropped out of American planes to rescue about 300 hostages being held in Stanleyville's Victoria Hotel. The hostages were made up of missionaries, embassy and business people. About twenty-seven of the hostages were killed and about fifty wounded just moments before the paratroopers reached them. One of those killed was American missionary doctor, Paul Carlson. Over the next two days, over 1800 Belgians, Americans, and other European nationals, along with over 300 Congolese were evacuated to Leopoldville. Major Mike Hoare's No. 5 Commando ANC* column of mostly South African, Rhodesian and Belgian mercenaries hired by Prime Minister Tshombe, arrived shortly after the paratroopers landed and helped secure the area. From there, and after the paratroopers had left, the mercenaries went through the rest of the rebel-held territory and rescued hundreds of other foreigners from remote mission stations, plantations, mining operations and government posts, including the family at Poko. In the madness that ensued after the paratroopers dropped in Stanleyville and Paulis, no person with any sort of ties to a foreign country was safe.)
* *Armee Nationale du Congo (Congolese National Army)*

November 26
Paratroopers came down on Paulis to rescue hostages. We heard that night that nineteen whites, including one missionary, were beaten to death in Paulis the day before. Two of our

children cried when they heard the news and our hearts were sad, as we knew this missionary well.

These hostages were killed in retaliation for the Stanleyville operation. American Jay Tucker died a horrible death that night, the second of thirteen according to his wife's report. She and the family were rescued on November 26 during the Paulis paratroop drop (Dragon Noir) which rescued many (though certainly not all) of the hostages in the area.

Aubrey's good friend Colin Buckley, is quoted in a story from the New York Times after being liberated in the Paulis para-operation, and one can feel his anguish knowing we were two hours away and the Ibambi folks about an hour away. But the troops and planes had been ordered to pull out (link in the blog).

November 27

When the rebels in Poko heard of the Paulis rescue operation only two hours away by road, they retaliated by having the Belgian prisoners taken out of prison. Their hands were tied behind their backs, and they were thrown on the ground, beaten and then left out in the hot sun. The rebels wanted to kill them but the Captain refused to let them. The local chief was shot.* We heard the shot and wondered if they were doing away with the hostages. A little while afterwards, four rebels came up to our house with spears, clubs and machetes. We wondered what they would do to us. Psalm 27:2** We greeted them and asked them to sit down on the veranda. They seemed angry and didn't have much to say. We gave them coffee and bread with margarine. After half an hour they got up and went away. We were relieved.

This was Chief Ekifulu whom Aubrey and Hulda had befriended. Ken remembers him having a 1958 Chevrolet car, one of the few cars in the area and an obvious sign of his wealth and status.

** *"When the wicked came against me to eat up my flesh, my enemies and foes, they stumbled and fell".*

November 28

A big truck drove up on our yard. The driver asked if he could leave it there. We had heard that rebels were running off with hostages, and wondered if the reason for the truck on our compound, was to have it ready to take us away before the National Army could rescue us. At ten after seven that evening, we had a frightening experience when there was a knock on our door. It was dark and two rebels asked to enter our house. After refusing them they began to get angry and were going to call others, so I opened the door and let them in. We did not fully know what they intended to do to us. We believe there was a Restraining Hand preventing them from harming us - because someone prayed. After three-quarters of an hour they got up and said, "If any Simba comes during the night, we must immediately open the door." Then they left. We spent most of that night in prayer as we didn't know what to expect. We were in extreme danger. But prayer changes things! Half the rebels fled from Poko that night while we were praying. We also asked the Lord to remove the truck and sure enough Sunday morning they came and got the truck.

November 29
We had a quiet Sunday. We stayed in our house all day and had special prayer. The Congolese on the station held their meetings. In the evening, we called the station people to come to our veranda and had a time of singing, fellowship and prayer. We did not know then, that this meeting would be our last time with them. Nor did they. But God did.

November 30
This day we shall never forget. The morning was fairly quiet. Our Simba guard came near midday. He had a gun and a spear. He continually denounced the white people. At 12:30 pm he left and said he would return at 4 pm. But God intervened. At 1:30 pm we heard shooting about two miles away where we knew there was a road block. A few minutes later there was a barrage of gun fire at the Government Post where the thirteen hostages were in prison. We shuttered our windows and locked the doors as we didn't yet know if friends or enemies had come. Soon a jeep and truck approached our house shooting in the air as they came to frighten the rebels. They pulled up outside our door and shouted "Come out, you're safe!" What welcome words! We came out and gave thanks to God and to them.

They were mostly Belgian soldiers - a volunteer ground unit of thirty brave men risking their lives to save others. Christians, learn from them! Are we willing to risk our lives to save the souls of others?

They gave us a few minutes to pack four suitcases as that was all we could take on the plane. Then they took us to the Government Post where we waited until they gathered up sixty-five other whites. Several times we lay on the floor in one of the buildings because of the bullets flying around us. We saw sweat, blood and tears. None of the mercenaries were killed. At 3:30 pm we were ready to move off in a convoy of six jeeps and four army trucks. We learned from some of the others that were rescued, that the rebels intended to take all of the whites at 4 pm that day to Paulis to be executed. But God had stepped in because you prayed. After about an hour on the road, some rebels started following us, but their truck was soon captured and they escaped into the forest. After three hours of travelling, we arrived at the town of Dingila.

December 1 to 3

We stayed here three days waiting for a plane. We didn't feel too safe as were still in rebel territory. On December 3 at 2 pm a plane arrived and twenty-four of us were flown to Leopoldville. The other 150 refugees were flown out from Dingila the following day. We didn't know until we arrived in Leopoldville that two of our fellow missionaries* had been killed in Stanleyville, and another two, both young men**, had been killed at Wamba.

Muriel Harman from Vancouver, BC and Cyril Taylor from New Zealand
**Bill McChesney from Phoenix, Arizona and Jim Rodger from Scotland*
Read their stories in the Photo Gallery: Congo Uprising album in the blog.

Our deliverance was a miracle and all who prayed played a big part in our being rescued. From August 25 to November 30, we were completely shut off from the outside world. We were thrilled and praise God for what we saw in the Congolese Christians. The two men who helped us in our home as well as the pastor and many students all stayed on the station with us at the risk of their own lives until we were rescued, whereas in the town of Poko all the people had fled to the forest during those last couple of days. We fear for what may have happened to the station people after we were gone. So, pray for the Christians. Not all the Congolese were rebels; it is a matter of the minority trying to rule the masses. The local population of Poko disliked the rebels.

We arrived in Canada on December 15 after spending six days at our mission headquarters near Philadelphia. It has been a sudden change for us in various ways. We are staying at the above address. We don't know yet what we shall do.

The Lord will guide. The children have started school this week here in Swift Current.

Sincerely yours in Him,
Aubrey and Hulda Brown

The stories of the WEC Congo missionaries from this time, are told in a small book "This Is No Accident" edited by Len Moules and long out of print. Aubrey's story is Chapter 13. WEC was just one of the mission societies affected. Many other groups, both Protestant and Catholic lost personnel as well, not to mention the many Belgian, Greek, and Portuguese plantation owners and traders, tribal chiefs and Congolese working in administrative or educational positions, many of whom were brutally executed. More than two hundred foreigners and thousands of Congolese were casualties of this one conflict - the Simba Rebellion, which was part of the greater five-year period of unrest known as the Congo Crisis following the country's independence, 1960 - 1965. A free download of This Is No Accident is available here:
https://www.smashwords.com/extreader/read/361095/1/this-is-no-accident
Aubrey picks up his memoir at this point and continues writing, relating the trip back to Canada.

"*The Lord was there,*" Ezekiel 35:10. He is always there. The rebels were blind and in darkness, as is everyone who has not received Christ into their hearts and followed Him.

What the rebels intended to do to us, and what really happened, were two different things. Why? Because "the Lord was there". God is in the heart, holding for Himself that for which He redeemed. He saw in those three months of 1964 during our captivity in the house on the hill at Poko, six lives that would in future days move out in Christian service. Every hour of everyday "the Lord was there".

The mercenaries rescued us at Poko from the hands of the rebels on November 30, 1964.

We lost everything except the four suitcases the mercenaries allowed us to take. As we were leaving Poko, the mercenaries found our Chevrolet Carryall that the rebels had taken from us, and added it to the convoy. But when it broke down, they burnt it so the rebels couldn't use it again.

After five days in Leopoldville, doing business and arranging air travel, we left for Canada on December 8. Menno Travel Service issued our tickets with an agreement that our mission headquarters would refund them on our arrival home.

We had a stopover in Athens for a short time where we took the time to walk all around the airport. It was great to be free!

The next stop was Brussels, and on the way, I remember looking out the window and seeing the mountains in Switzerland covered with snow as we crossed Europe. Word had been sent ahead saying that provision of clothes should be made available for the refugees from Congo, as we had no clothes for winter.

When we got off the plane in Brussels, the Red Cross folks came running out to meet us on the tarmac with coats and sweaters. How kind of them! Once inside the air terminal, I was approached by someone who introduced himself as the Australian Ambassador to Belgium. He was notified that some Australians were arriving and to offer assistance if needed. He asked me if I needed anything and I told him I needed warm underwear. He said he would look for some and soon came back with a parcel that contained underwear which was just the right size for me. People in Brussels were so kind to us and gave us what we needed to face the cold weather ahead of us.

Leaving Brussels, we flew to New York and as we passed over England the sun was going down. Hour after hour it seemed to stay put in the sky as we travelled west over the Atlantic. That day seemed to never end.

Our mission friends were at the airport in New York to meet us. We stayed at the WEC American headquarters in Fort Washington, Pennsylvania for six days. My friend Arthur Mathews* of the Overseas Missionary Fellowship came to see us one evening. A Presbyterian church group nearby, upon hearing of our arrival, invited us to a clothing shower for us. It was really wonderful how the Lord supplied our need.

* Arthur Matthews was Aubrey's friend from Melbourne Bible Institute.

From headquarters, Hulda phoned her brother Henry who was the pastor of an Alliance church in Morden, Manitoba. He insisted that we stop in Winnipeg and meet the people who prayed for our release and safety.

Leaving New York, we flew to Toronto where it took us a while to get through immigration. When everything was settled, we flew to Winnipeg where Pastor Henry and Elaine Schroeder were waiting to meet us. They took us to their home in Morden and arranged a meeting for us in their church, where we were asked to tell the story of our rescue. A reporter was present and our story was published the next day in both the local newspaper and the Winnipeg newspaper.*

* An audio recording of this evening's talk was also made for a radio broadcast and is available in the Audio Archives link in The Long Road blog.

Our next stop on our way home was Regina where some of Hulda's folks were living. We were taken to a television station where they interviewed us about the recent events in Congo.

The final trip was from Regina to Waldheim in Saskatchewan where Hulda's mother and two sisters were. By this time, it was nearly Christmas and we were happy to spend the season in Waldheim with loved ones.

And that ended the eventful year of 1964.

THE BROWN FAMILY ARRIVES HOME SAFELY IN CANADA, LATE 1964
PHOTO COURTESY OF WINNIPEG FREE PRESS ARCHIVES

Chapter 8

Third Furlough
1965 to 1971

FAMILY PORTRAIT IN VANCOUVER, 1970

Canada

1965 to 1971

Early in January of 1965, we moved into the house of Hulda's mother in Swift Current. We hadn't been there long when I received a telegram from Australia. It read something like this: "Mother passed away peacefully this morning. Rupert." This was a shock to me as I had not heard that she was ill.

Mother died in Bendigo on January 14th, 1965, at the age of 83. She was a godly woman and I thank God for every remembrance of her. Early in life she won prizes for Scripture memorization, she loved attending the weekly Christian Endeavor meetings and took a very active part in them.

In Swift Current, our four children had to face new schools again. Ron went to High School and the other three attended another school. It was cold for them walking to school in the winter time.

We attended the Christian & Missionary Alliance church. The people there were kind and helpful. They gave us a gift of money at one of the services. In early February, I was invited to speak at the C&MA Bible College* in Regina.

This college would eventually move to Calgary, join with the Nazarene College and by 2007 it would become known as Ambrose University.

Later on in the year, Hulda's mother and sister returned to their home and we were happy to stay with them until we found a suitable house to buy. I was out holding meetings in different churches and sometimes I was away from the family for weeks at a time. The longest period was on a deputation

141

tour that lasted three months in 1965. It was arranged by the western representative of the mission in the United States. I was included on a team with two other missionaries who had been rescued by mercenaries in Congo during the rebellion. We held meetings in various churches right down the coast from Vancouver to Los Angeles and then eastward into the state of Arizona. In Phoenix, we stayed with and visited the parents of Bill McChesney, a young missionary who was killed by the rebels in Congo. They had arranged meetings in schools and churches for us and had given some of Bill's slides for us to use.

During this time when I was away, Hulda's brother Vic helped her to buy a house not far away from her mother's home. I was able to send home some money for Hulda to buy furniture. When I arrived back in Swift Current, I was taken to our new home at 10 Gibbs Street. It was great to be back with the family after three months on the road. Christmas Day in 1965 was a big event with the large Schroeder family gathering in Swift Current to celebrate.

In 1966, we were asked by the mission to do deputation work and visit Bible Schools. We had purchased an old Nash car the previous year, but one day it stopped and went no more. Hulda's brother lent us his car for a while and in April we drove to Three Hills to attend the Prairie Bible Institute's spring conference and graduation. From there we visited Briercrest Bible School and then Pambrun Bible School. We covered 1000 miles visiting these three schools.

When we returned to Swift Current, we found a 1957 Meteor car for sale which we bought and it did us very good service.

In July when the children were out of school, we drove our Meteor across to Fort Washington in Pennsylvania where our US mission headquarters was situated on Camp Hill. It was the annual mission conference for all the home staff workers and missionaries on furlough. It was a real blessing to meet up with our fellow workers.

After conference we left and drove north 450 miles to the state of Maine. I had been in Maine a year or so before, holding meetings and at one home where I had stayed, they had invited me to come and spend a few days anytime and to bring my family as they had an extra cabin on their yard. So, I took them up on the offer and stayed at the cabin that was only a couple of blocks from the Atlantic Ocean and we so enjoyed the times on the beach.

After five days rest and relaxation there we made our way home to Swift Current arriving back on August 16th after covering 6700 miles. Ron did most of the driving and did a good job. After we were home, he went to his uncle's farm* in Main Centre and worked until school started.

Jake and Margaret Schroeder

In September, I arranged a speaking tour for a missionary couple from Java, Indonesia, as well as one for myself. This meant writing letters to pastors and Bible Schools and trying to arrange meetings so that travelling costs would be at a minimum.

I set out for meetings in Manitoba from October 5 to October 31. I visited Winnipeg and had good meetings there. From there, I spoke in Chapel at Winnipeg Bible College and then I went to Steinbach and spoke for twenty minutes at the Steinbach Bible Institute chapel. The students wanted to hear more about Congo so they arranged for me to speak another twenty minutes over their noon hour. From there I had meetings on the way up north as far as Swan River* and then back to Virden.

Aubrey couldn't have known then, that on a farm just east of the town, there lived a little six-year-old girl who would grow up to become his daughter-in-law.

In November, I did a tour south across the border into the United States, to Montana. The second day of this tour I got caught up in a blizzard. It was snowing with fierce winds. I had a difficult time that day to find my way as the road signs were covered with snow and it was a new road to me. However, the Lord protected me and helped me find the pastor's place and we had a good meeting in his church. The following day, I found the roads were icy and that slowed me down. On this tour, I visited one of Hulda's brothers* who was pastoring a church at a place called Ronan, and he had arranged meetings for me.

Art and Vi Schroeder

During the latter part of 1966, I noticed that I couldn't see as well as I used to. I visited a doctor in Regina and he couldn't see much wrong with my eyes.

While I was away on deputation, Hulda was caring for the children and at times was helping her sister Emma take care of their mother who was very ill and had been for some time. On December 5th at 2:30 pm, Hulda's mother went to be with the Lord at the age of 82. Her earthly pilgrimage was now over. She was a mother to fifteen children and a grandma to over thirty grandchildren.

In early 1967, we started thinking of moving again. Ron was finishing his last year of High School and after he graduated he wanted to enter Bible School. Prairie Bible Institute was a good school in Three Hills, Alberta; it was where Hulda attended many years ago and we had just visited there. It had a strong missions emphasis and would be a good place for me to be based as I continued to represent WEC. So, we decided to move and I made a trip to Three Hills with a friend to look for a place.

We looked at several houses and lots and decided to buy a lot at 209 2nd Avenue North. It was close to the Bible School and close to the town. We ordered a pre-fabricated house package from Nelson Homes in Lloydminster. Then I returned to Swift Current, after making a down payment on the lot. Applications were made for all four children to enter schools at Prairie and then we put our house up for sale in Swift Current.

David's Grade 5 classes were due to start on August 28, so I took him to Three Hills and he started school. We both stayed with friends* who looked after a large boarding home for missionary children called the WEC Home. It was one mile north of town. Hulda stayed with the other three children in Swift Current until our house was sold and then the rest of the family moved to Three Hills in early September.

* Herb and Marion Congo

Our pre-fab house was delivered and it took four men about six hours to unload. The construction began on August 23rd and we moved into the basement on December 16th and lived there until the main floor was finished. A missionary friend* did the building and I helped where I could. My eyesight was getting worse and it was difficult to pound nails.

* Stan Christon

My daily schedule during those last four months of 1967 was as follows: I would leave the WEC Home where we were staying to go to work on our house at 7:20 am. I would take Ron along to his first class. The other children would walk the mile to school and at noon, I would bring them home. I went back to work at 1 pm and dropped the children off at school. Then I would come home after work at 5:30 or 6 pm It was so nice to be all together in our new home by mid-December, 1967.

In that same month of December, as we were just settling in Three Hills, we received a letter from our mission headquarters in Australia. At their quarterly conference they had decided to ask us to come and take over the mission headquarters in Victoria. As our children had just settled into school, we felt another move was out of the question at this time.

At the end of that year, I went to see the local doctor and after examining my eyes, he sent me to a specialist in Calgary who told me that I had cataracts on both eyes. He told me to wait a while until they developed further as they were not ready to be operated on yet.

Our move to another province didn't change my job description. I was still the mission representative for the three prairie provinces: Manitoba, Saskatchewan, and Alberta. Although with my eyes failing so badly I could not go on tour myself, I was still able to arrange tours for others.

In early 1968, I had another appointment with the eye specialist in Calgary and he said I was now ready to have the cataracts removed, I just had to wait once more until a hospital bed was available.

One day in April I was sitting with a friend in the Prairie Tabernacle listening to a visiting speaker at the Spring Conference. Someone came in and called me out of the meeting. I was told that the specialist in Calgary had phoned and asked me to go to the General Hospital in Calgary to prepare for eye surgery.

My one eye was operated on April 9 and six days later the surgeon removed the cataract from the other eye. I was in hospital for fifteen days. The doctor tested my eyes and gave me a pair of dark glasses to wear as my eyes healed. He told me I had 15/20 vision and the operations were successful. I was so happy and thankful that I could see properly once more. Two months later, I had my eyes tested again and the doctor gave me a very thick pair of glasses, which enabled me to read. Later on in the year the doctor tested my eyes again and I received hard contact lens.

During the summer months when the children began their summer holidays, we decided that Hulda should take Ken, David and another boy* to Yarrow in British Columbia. Friends of ours grew raspberries in large fields and needed help harvesting them. Ken had just received his license to drive the car and he drove through the Rocky Mountains and back again without incident. Ron and Carol were both working elsewhere during the summer. I stayed home and kept busy painting the outside of the house.

* Jon Hines was a fellow WEC missionary kid also attending school in Three Hills. His parents worked in Columbia and he was like an honorary brother.

In August, I tried for my driver's license and after receiving it, I was so happy to be able to sit behind the wheel of a car again after a year of not driving. I drove to Calgary to pick up Carol who was returning from working in Banff for the summer.

When school started again in September, Carol and Ken started grade eleven in Three Hills High School. Hulda and I did a week's short tour up in the Peace River country, northwest from Three Hills. This is good wheat growing country. We had meetings in Fort St. John, Spirit River, Hines Creek, Peace River and at the Bible School in Sexmith. We had one more meeting at Whitecourt on our way home.

In the Bible we read in Ecclesiastes 11, verses 1 and 6: *Cast thy bread upon the waters for thou shalt find it after many days. In the morning sow thy seed, and in the evening withhold not thy hand: for thou knowest not whether shall prosper, either this or that, or whether they both shall be alike good.*

One can never tell the results of the many meetings where one has given the challenge of the great commission to *Go into all the world and preach the Gospel to every creature.** What has been the response? Perhaps we shall never know, but from the many books bought and pamphlets taken from those meetings, we have trusted the Lord to use His Word to bring believers to a place where they are ready to go to any place and to do anything to minister whether here at home or in a foreign field.

*Mark 16:15

I set off again in November on another tour starting at Didsbury Bible School and then going up into northern Alber-

146

ta. This took me a whole month. On arriving home in Three Hills, I received a phone call from the pastor of the Baptist Church in Trochu asking me if I could take the morning and evening services in his church as he was laid aside with sickness. We went as a family and all took part in the services on December 15th, 1968.

The year of 1969 was spent with going on several deputation tours myself, as well as arranging tours for other missionaries. For me it was fulfilling work. Hulda stayed at home and cared for the family while we were separated for weeks at a time.

The Lord had increasingly burdened my heart for those without Christ and especially for those who had never had a chance to ever hear the Gospel because no one cared enough to take it to them. In deputation meetings one had the opportunity to bring the needs of the unevangelized fields of the world before the Christian Church. In these meetings I could challenge Christians, especially young people, to consider going to the needy mission fields and to ask the older people to pray and support others.

One sees the hundred years that the Moravian churches sent out missionaries and the sacrifice and the impact they made in the world in their time. We, in our churches today, pale in comparison to the zeal of the Moravians. Many Christians choose an easy life and are not interested in missionary work. The motto of the Moravian church always appealed to me. It was an illustration that showed a bullock standing between an altar and a plough and underneath was the inscription that read "Ready for either—sacrifice or service." Our WEC mission motto by C.T. Studd was something similar: "If Jesus Christ be God and died for me then no sacrifice can be too great for me to make for Him."

I was not only interested in the thirty or so countries where our mission was working, but I became interested in many missionary societies, churches and Bible Colleges which were all working with a vision to see needy tribes and nations in other parts of the world have an opportunity to hear the gospel so that they could respond to the words of the Lord Jesus, "Come unto Me".

These were some of the thoughts in my mind as I travelled from church to church, from school to school across the prairie

147

provinces. In the meetings as I stood up to speak I would think, "Who in this place will make his or her life a living sacrifice, and be available to the Lord of the Harvest? Who will respond saying, 'Here am I, send me'?"

In February and March, I had meetings in Bassano, Gem, Tilley and Medicine Hat in Baptist, Alliance, and EFC churches. On to Maple Creek, Gull Lake, Shaunavon, Pambrun (Millar Memorial Bible Institute), Vanguard, Gouldtown, Main Center, Briercrest Bible College, Moose Jaw, Regina, Canadian Bible College, Davidson, Outlook, Kindersley, Acadia Valley, and Coronation. At Coronation, we all went as a family from Three Hills and took part in the Sunday morning and evening services.

During April, I was usually at the spring missionary conference of Prairie Bible Institute. All the mission representatives, myself included, would set up tables with displays, books and curios. In this way we made contacts with students and visitors between meetings. Each mission was given a room where they could hold a seminar for those interested.

In May, Hulda went to Swift Current for eleven days to be with her sister who was very ill with cancer. I kept busy at home preparing meals for the children and planting a garden. There was good black soil behind our house and I planted potatoes and lots of vegetable seeds. I loved working in the garden and watching the young plants come up and grow. Man plants but God gives the increase.

Carol had five piano students coming to the house after school and gave them music lessons, one each day.

When Hulda returned home, I set out on May 27 and did a tour of meetings in British Columbia, starting in Bellevue. I had a missionary film which I showed quite often depicting conflict and conquest in Columbia as the early missionaries preached the gospel. Many people in South America responded and became Christians back then in the thirties and forties. I also showed slides of our work in Congo and sold literature. The next stop was Creston and from there I had a meeting in a Covenant church at Wynndel. From there I spoke in Trail, Grand Forks, Greenwood, Midway, Oliver, Kelowna, Vernon, Salmon Arm and then back home.

One Sunday in July, our family went down to Black Diamond, south of Calgary, for a morning and evening service where we all took part. I was asked to speak at Prairie Tabernacle at the evening service of September 7 and I spoke on Psalm 85:6 and shared about the 1953 revival that took place in Congo.

After the Bible School students returned for another year of Bible study in September, a fall conference is generally held in October at Prairie Bible Institute. What a blessing it is to listen to visiting speakers and missionaries on furlough and mission representatives from all parts of the world. Following this conference came more deputation and Christmas with the family.

Early in 1970, I wrote to pastors of churches and to Bible Schools in Saskatchewan to see if they would be interested in arranging meetings for a team of three missionaries. They were missionaries on furlough from different countries - Thailand, Iran, and Borneo. I received favourable replies and I arranged a few meetings for myself.

The day came when these three men arrived in Three Hills. After a week of meetings at Prairie Bible Institute and in churches around this area, we were ready to take off. The four of us drove to Calgary's Berean Bible Institute and had a chapel service there. Then east to Medicine Hat's Hillcrest Bible School, then Briercrest Bible Institute, Miller Memorial Bible Institute, and Swift Current Bible Institute; a total of six Bible schools. We would set up an interesting table with literature and curios from overseas countries and in this way contacted many interested students. The three men went on eastward for further meetings by bus, and as we separated I headed north for another fifteen meetings before returning to Three Hills.

I returned in time for the annual spring missionary conference and graduation at PBI. Arthur Mathews of Overseas Missionary Fellowship was one of the visiting speakers and I was thrilled to meet him again. He was a friend and classmate at Melbourne Bible Institute back in 1935-1937 and I had gone to the ship to say good-bye to him when he first left for missionary work in China. His book, *Green Leaf in Drought*, which he wrote after he got out of prison and returned from China, was a great blessing to me and to many other people.

Then it was time to plant the garden and I began to arrange meetings closer to home. In this way I could take Hulda and the family for Sunday services.

By the summer of 1970, Hulda and I had been praying and seeking the Lord's mind about our return to Congo. In view of this we planned to do a month-long tour with the four children during the summer. I wrote to some pastors and friends whom I had met on another tour down the west coast of the United States, and asked them if they would be interested in arranging meetings for us. Most of them replied favorably.

With all arranged, we started off on July 21 and returned August 22. First, we went west to British Colombia, right out to the city of Vancouver on the coast, taking meetings along the way and visiting relatives and friends. We then turned south into the United States, holding meetings in Washington, Oregon and California. Hulda's sister Mary and her husband* lived in Reedley, California at that time and we stayed six days with them, having some meetings in that area. Then we drove on to Phoenix in Arizona. That was a terribly hot day as we drove through the desert for nearly 400 miles. It was 105 degrees Fahrenheit. We knew a family in Phoenix whose son had been a missionary with us in Congo. We stayed with the McChesney's who had arranged some meetings for us. I spoke to the High School students in the school that Bill McChesney had attended a few years previous. Most of the houses and cars had air conditioning, but our car didn't so what couldn't be cured had to be endured.

Mary and Henry Penner, who were also kind enough to take the family to Disneyland

From Phoenix we drove north and saw the Grand Canyon and from there on to Salt Lake City where the Mormons have their headquarters. That day we covered 660 miles. Ron did most of the driving with Ken and Carol taking turns. I drove once, I remember, when Ron got sleepy. Our good friends at Salt Lake City took us to their evangelical church for a meeting and showed us around the city. Our children went for a swim in the salt lake.

From there we drove on to Yellowstone Park. Just right near the Park our car broke down and we had to stay two days in a motel until it was fixed. We made it home to Three Hills and thanked the Lord for a safe trip and His good hand upon those who drove.

When Bible school started again in September they had a goodly number of students, around 750. In October was the usual fall conference and we heard good messages from Roy Hession and Ivor Powell.

During November, one Sunday morning we all left very early and drove south 150 miles for the morning service in Picture Butte where we all took part. We had two other meetings and then drove home. That was a long and tiring day.

When I was working in my office downstairs, I was able to hear the speakers at the chapel service over campus radio line. I could hear Mr. Maxwell speaking on Revelation and remembered Ron was in that class because this was his last year at Bible School.

That fall we received a letter from our field director in Congo. Mr. Scholes had just visited Poko station where we had worked up until 1964. He told us that the Africans would give us a great welcome if and when we returned. Our thoughts were certainly turning that way.

I spoke again to the PBI students in a chapel service on December 11th from Psalm 116 on the benefits of being a child of God.

Just before Christmas, most of the students would leave to spend Christmas with their families. Ron went to the large student conference in Urbana, Illinois with a carload from Prairie. This was a great experience for the thousands of young people who were able to attend. Carol left for work in a motel in Banff and Ken went to work on a farm.

About this time, we made inquiries to see if Dave could enter Grade Nine at Rethy Academy back in the Congo for the coming year. We also made inquiries to see if he could do his high school at Kijabe in Kenya. Then we began the process of putting our house up for sale and applied for visas to return to Congo.

While these things were taking place, I was overseeing a job at the home for missionaries' children where we had lived when our house was being built. A drilling rig came on to the yard to bore for water and they found water at 170 feet. They put down a five-inch pipe with a submersible pump at the end and water could be then be pumped up from the well into the cistern in the basement.

When the winter was nearly over in 1971, the usual tour of meetings began. In March I went up into Northern Alberta and then eastward into Saskatchewan as far as Nipawin. Returning to Three Hills, I had arranged meetings along the way. I had a film with me called *Africa Heartbeat* which I showed at some of the meetings.

Ron was graduating in April and he had sent an invitation to my sister in Australia to come to his graduation from Bible College. I never expected her to come to Three Hills, but she really surprised us when we received a letter to say she was coming. In early April, we all went to Calgary airport to meet her. This was a happy day for me to see Gladys again after we had been separated for nearly nine years. We had lots to talk about and we enjoyed her stay of nine weeks with us.

During April we enjoyed the spring missionary conference at PBI and especially the graduation day when we saw Ron along with many others receiving their diplomas from the president of the college, Rev. L.E. Maxwell.

After graduation, we went to Swift Current for a wedding. It was Hulda's sister Emma, who was getting married to a pastor from the United States. Gladys came along with us. One Sunday morning we took her out to Main Centre to the morning service in the church where Hulda attended when she was living at home on the farm and until she left home to work and prepare for missionary work in Africa.

Our house was up for sale and one day our pastor came to the door with an elderly couple. We showed them around and they liked the house and decided to buy it. We had to be out of the house by June 15, so we decided to move back into the WEC Home, where we were staying during the building of this home which we had just sold at 209 2nd Avenue North.

A friend came up from Calgary and crated our piano so we could take with us to Africa. When all our crates were packed, nailed down and banded, they were shipped to HQ in Philadelphia.

With the money received from selling our house we were able to purchase a Chevrolet three-quarter-ton truck in New York. We did this in May when we went to our headquarters in Philadelphia for a conference. We packed a few more things and our freight left for Mombasa, Kenya on August 17. The boat stopped at New York and our truck was loaded on three days later.

On our way home from conference we drove home in a car that a couple asked us to take back to Three Hills. They were missionaries and had just left to return to Ivory Coast. We were able to visit with relatives and friends along the way and say our good-byes to some of them before we reached Three Hills safely.

We had our farewells and picked up David and started back to Congo. The president of the country had just changed the name of the country in the last few months and the new name was Zaire. We wondered what else had changed in the time we had been away.

It wasn't easy saying goodbye to the other three children at Calgary airport. We had been in Canada six-and-a-half years since the rebellion in 1964. The last four years were spent in Alberta and the previous two-and-a-half years in Saskatchewan.

Our fourth term was about to begin in Zaire.

THE BROWN FAMILY IN THREE HILLS, 1971

Chapter 9

Fourth Term
1971 to 1975

AUBREY AND HULDA'S BIBLE SCHOOL CLASS, 1974

CHECKING BRIDGES BEFORE CROSSING, 1973

Poko and Mulita

1971 to 1975

On September 2, we left Calgary and flew to Amsterdam. After one night there, we went on to Entebbe airport in Uganda flying with Raptim.* Two missionaries with Africa Inland Mission met us and took us to Kampala. Dave left us after a few days and travelled into Zaire and on to Rethy Academy with a couple (Arnold and Shirley Olver) who were house parents at the MK school. He had to be there by September 7 to start Grade 9.

* This was the first time Aubrey and Hulda had used the humanitarian not-for-profit Dutch travel agency.

Hulda stayed at the Namirembe Guest House in Kampala run by the Anglican Church Missionary Society, while I took the train from Kampala to Mombasa to pick up the truck and our freight. I was put into a carriage (train car) with two African students from Makerere University and one white professor from the university. It was a different Africa now that most countries had received their independence from colonial rule.

When I arrived in Mombasa, I was able to pick up our truck which had just arrived. After a day or so I was able to get our crates and the piano out of customs and loaded onto the truck. It was late in the day as I drove back to the hotel. I went to the authorities and asked them for a guard to watch over the truck and freight while I slept. Thieves couldn't carry the piano away but might be tempted to steal other things.

I was up early next morning and after breakfast, I paid the guard and started off on my way to Kampala. I thought that I might stop in Nairobi for the night, but when I arrived there, the sun was still high in the sky and so after filling up with gas I drove on until sundown. At one place soldiers in a jeep passed me and after a little while they had stopped and were waiting for me. They stared at me, but didn't stop me. After a few minutes they passed me again and I never saw them after that. When I arrived at Nakuru I found a hotel where I stayed for the night. After I had eaten, I phoned Hulda in Kampala to let her know I was on the way and DV* would arrive next day.

Deo Volente - Latin for 'God willing'

Arriving at the border between Kenya and Uganda, I was held up for a while at customs, but the Lord enabled me to have a good trip and to arrive safely at Namirembe. This was the third vehicle I had driven along this road - one in 1953 from Mombasa, one in 1962 from Nairobi, and now one from Mombasa in 1971.

1952 Chevrolet 3100 half-ton pickup, 1961 Opel station wagon, 1971 Chevrolet C/20 three-quarter ton pickup.

Things were tense in Kampala and we were glad to get out of there. We had business to do before we left, and by the time we filled up with gas, we didn't get an early start.

Early in the afternoon the gauge showed we would soon have to fill up with gas again. We were looking for a gas station but couldn't see any sign of one. Then we saw a sign leading into a tourist resort so we followed the road in and we were able to fill up with gas.

The bad news was we noticed one suitcase was missing from the back of the truck. We were not sure whether it had been stolen when we stopped to eat at noon or whether it had fallen off the truck. We drove back to see if we could find it but there was no suitcase alongside the road. This made our hearts heavy as we continued on towards Zaire.

Hulda recounts in her book that the suitcase contained most of their clothes for this term.

The sun was nearly down when we crossed the Nile River and we decided to stop for the night at Pakwach. We went to one hotel but decided not to sleep there so we went back to the soldiers' camp we had passed on entering the town. It looked safer for us to camp with the soldiers. We asked permission to do so and they kindly agreed. What a horrible night we had. If we shut the windows of the truck up tight it was too hot to sleep and if we opened them just a little to get some air, the mosquitos came in. They were there in the hundreds. We hardly had any sleep and longed for daybreak. We were so tired and heavy-hearted at losing our good clothes which were in the suitcase that was missing.

When morning came, we said goodbye to the Ugandan soldiers and set off for Rethy. We crossed into Zaire and passed through customs at Mahagi, arriving at Rethy at noon. The folks there were having lunch and we were invited to join them. We were happy to see Dave again.

By this time, I was beat and had to go to bed to rest for a while.

We stayed a day or two at Rethy where I was able to buy a forty-litre drum and fill it with gas because gas was scarce in Zaire at this time.

We said good-bye to Dave and the kind friends at Rethy and set off for Ibambi. We drove all day and because of bad roads, we arrived after dark at the Watsa mission station. The folks had been waiting for us and had supper ready for us. In the morning they sold us some gas and we drove to another Africa Inland Mission station at Dungu. The Greeks in the town sold us gas and we left the next day for Isiro. The road now was familiar, as I had travelled over these roads many times when I lived at Niangara and had trekked in this area before I was married. We bypassed Niangara and drove down to Isiro where our friends, Colin and Ina Buckley were living on the outskirts of Isiro at Gamba mission station. When we were driving into Isiro a policeman stopped us and said our load was too high on the truck and we didn't have side mirrors on the truck. I had taken the mirrors off the truck in New York as well as the hub caps and they were somewhere packed away in the back of the truck. Anyway, the police let us go on to Gamba. We unloaded some of our stuff and found the mirrors and put them back on. These often get stolen when trucks are unloaded at the ports.

After a day or so at Gamba, we drove down to Ibambi to visit the field director to get our new assignment for this new term. He told us that the field council had decided we should return to Poko where we had been rescued by mercenaries about seven years previously. We were happy to go back there and felt in our hearts it was God's will.

That was a memorable day, the day we left Ibambi to go to Poko. We picked up some of the things we had unloaded at Gamba, did some shopping in Isiro and started for Poko. The roads were bad. When we came into Poko area the villages were familiar. We arrived and stopped at a church called Nero. There the pastor received us with joy and emotion. He said he hadn't expected us to ever return to Zaire. What a great welcome the Christians gave us.

We drove on to Poko and driving up the hill to our mission station we wondered how we would be received. Not knowing where would we live, we pulled up in the shade of a big mango tree by the church and soon we were surrounded by welcome hand-shakes and great joy. The long journey was now over.

The pastor took us into the house from where the mercenaries had rescued the six of us on November 30th. Congolese had been living in the house and hadn't left it very clean. However, we were glad to be back, and here we were among friends and fellow believers. Some men came and helped us unload the truck. We unloaded the piano into the front room and there it stayed crated up for several days until we had time to see to it. The Africans were eager to see what was in that big box. A day came when we took the piano out of the crate and put it in a corner of the living room and when Hulda played it, we found it in tune. We kept a small kerosene lamp burning in it because of the humidity and it gave us much enjoyment.

On our next trip back to Isiro, we picked up the rest of our crates at Gamba, and soon we were well settled into the work at Poko again.

This, our last term on the field, was three and a half years. We spent two and a half years at Poko and the last year at Mulita, one of our southern stations where there was a Bible School.

Regarding our settling into our house at Poko, yes, we had the house to ourselves - all except one room which was the office. The national pastor was reluctant to move out of the office and give us the key. It was rather annoying to have people coming into the house and passing through our living room and unlocking the door of the office and after a while going out again. We kept quiet for several months and prayed about the matter. Eventually the pastor moved his things out and then for us it was more privacy; the house was totally ours.

There is a spiritual lesson here. How many Christian people make a profession of faith in Christ and let Him in, but not to every room of their heart? There is a key to one room they will not yield; some secret sin that is not confessed. Later, because of conviction by the Holy Spirit, body, soul, and spirit are yielded to Christ and then peace and joy fills that person.

After we had received all the keys of the house, we felt free to lock up the house and start visiting some of the eighty churches in the Poko area. How thrilled the Congolese were to see us back and what stories they told us of their experiences during the rebellion of 1964.

Back on the station I was asked by the church leaders to start teaching students who had come on to the station from some of the region's churches. Their desire was to go to the *(Ibambi)* Bible School, but they needed to up-grade their education in order to pass the entrance exam for Bible School.

Two couples who came for training told us about their suffering when they had to flee to the forest for safety when the rebels attacked their village. They nearly starved to death. One of the wives I had known before the rebellion. Around the year 1963 I had been trekking in that area where she lived. I had not intended to visit the village where she lived because it was several miles from the motor road. The people insisted that I should come and teach them. I left the truck on the side of the road and told a Christian man to guard it while I was away. I gathered up a few carriers from a nearby church and we set off on foot and walked for several hours until we arrived in the village. We had good meetings and good attendance and souls came to the Lord. One young woman was especially bright for the Lord. Her name was Mivunguno. When she came on to the station, she had since married Yenga, and I recognized her immediately after not seeing her for eight years. This couple made it through Bible School and later Yenga and Mivunguno proved themselves faithful in the service of the Lord and the church ordained Yenga to be a pastor of a growing church where they have laboured for years.

Another story we heard was from a faithful teacher who pastored a village church, his name was Bakira. When the rebel soldiers came to arrest him in his house he escaped through the back door and fled to the grassland to hide. The rebel soldiers were furious and searched for him. Then they decided to set fire to the grass and surrounded the large patch of grass which was six to eight feet tall,* hoping Bakira would come out. Bakira knowing what was happening cried out to God. He said, "Oh God, you saved Daniel in the lions' den and you saved the three Hebrew men in the fiery furnace and now do the same for me!"

Elephant grass, sometimes called Napier or Uganda grass can be seen on page 67, the photograph from 1940 with Aubrey's porters walking in a line through this tall grass.

Bakira told us the flames came within a few feet of where he was hiding and then died down. There was still a tiny patch of grass left where he was hiding. The soldiers couldn't see him but he could see them leaving one by one presuming he was burnt in the fire. They thought they had achieved their goal, but alas for them, God still moves in mysterious ways His wonders to perform. After the rebels had left, Bakira crept out alive and well. He came to see us a few weeks after our arrival in Poko in 1971 and told us this story.

Another faithful teacher living near Poko found a coffee table which had been thrown away in the forest. He recognized the table that once had been in our living room. The rebels had stolen it, used it, and then dumped it when they fled. He brought it back to us along with our jack for the truck. This was from the truck the mercenaries had destroyed when they rescued us so that the rebels could not use it again.

One Congolese woman told us that in her dream she had seen Hulda and me, and was convinced that we were alive. Other rumors came to Poko that our whole family had been killed by the rebels after we left from their sight. They had no way of knowing what happened to us until a year or so after the rebellion.

When December came along it was time to make the three-hour trip to the airport at Isiro to meet Dave who was returning home from Rethy for the Christmas holidays.*

Dave's trips back and forth from Rethy to Isiro were possible because of the Mission Aviation Fellowship flights that were cost-effective alternatives to driving on the ever-worsening roads. Before the rebellion, these trips had taken six days for the round trip and had to be done three times a year. MAF operates worldwide, meeting the transportation and cargo needs of many missions and humanitarian groups in remote areas. They are still very active in Congo.

After we picked up Dave, we did some shopping and returned to Poko. Then we started to prepare for the Christmas conference, when the Christians and others came in from the eighty district churches What a time of rejoicing that was for us to see! And what a time of rejoicing for them to see us after an absence of seven years; little children who had been six and seven years old were now teenagers! During those days of conference in 1971 the Word was preached, souls were saved, backsliders were restored, believers were encouraged and some were baptized. When the conference ended after three days, with four meetings a day, and as evening drew near, the three of us took our evening meal and joined our African brothers and sisters and ate together with them our Christmas meal. What a blessing that was; all one in Christ Jesus!

Early in January of 1972 we took Dave back to Isiro to catch the MAF plane to the AIM* school at Rethy. He returned for a short break at Easter.

* *Africa Inland Mission*

During that time that Dave was with us, we visited a church at Kpo and moved a family who were voluntary workers to a needier area near Amadi. Then I went back to the Kpo church to pick up three married students who wanted to come to the preparatory school we had started at Poko.* In all, twelve to fifteen came on to the mission station to be taught. Meanwhile, Hulda supervised the Thursday women's meetings and the Sunday Schools. She would meet with the SS teachers during the week and go through the lesson with them. When they met on Sunday morning several classes would be held outside the church under the trees as there were not many classrooms.

* *This trip is the background to the story in the Family Tributes chapter of the blog.*

Early in that year, the field director sent a new missionary couple* to us at Poko and asked us to teach them the Bangala language before they moved further west to another station. We enjoyed their company and fellowship over several months. While with us, Howard built a back for our truck, cemented the area around the main water spring on the mission

163

station where our drinking water came from, and showed the workmen how to lay a cement floor in the large brick church.

Howard and Pam Burns from Durban, South Africa.

Putting a cement floor in the church at Poko was a project of the women's Thursday meetings. They gave offerings every week out of their poverty. The students I was teaching took out sand from the Bomakandi River nearby and I hauled it from the river to a room at the back of the church in our Chev truck. When the women had raised enough money, I would drive the three hours to Isiro and buy several sacks of cement. The students then would lay a section of the floor until the cement finished. We would have to wait then until the women raised more money and then do another section. Over the year the whole project was finished. The brick church at Poko now had a cement floor and an iron roof - a permanent building.* It was a building where much prayer was offered, a place where voices were raised to praise and exalt the Saviour, a place of preaching and teaching. It was God's House. "We love the place, O God, wherein Thine honour dwells; the joy of Thine abode, all earthly joy excels.**

The building still stands, as is shown in the screen shot from a recent satellite image and viewable in the blog. Within the circle, the church is the long rusty roof and Aubrey and Hulda's house was the darker roof to the left. The Bomakandi River at the top and on the far right is the town centre.

** *From the hymn "We Love The Place, O God" by William Bullock, 1854 - naval officer, Canadian missionary, Church of England clergyman, and hymn-writer from Halifax.*

When on the station I would teach the students and others from 6:30 to 7:30 every morning, Monday through Friday. On Sunday mornings there was always a prayer meeting at 7 am and another on Tuesday evenings. Sunday services started at 10 am and again in the afternoon at 3 pm. Most of the students would go out into the villages to preach and teach on Sundays.

At the end of June, it was time to make another trip to Isiro to meet Dave. He had completed his grade nine with success and was returning to Poko. As there was no high school at Rethy, we had originally expected that Dave would go along with his classmates to an AIM high school in Kijabe, Kenya. But as the political scene in Uganda was getting worse when Idi Amin was ruling that country, it was too dangerous to travel by road or fly across that country.

So, we made application then to Prairie High School back in Three Hills, Alberta and Dave was accepted. We then made preparations and a booking for his return to Canada by himself. We contacted a missionary in Kinshasa to meet him at the airport and see that he made his connecting flight to Belgium, and from there to Montreal and Calgary.

On the day that Dave was to arrive in Calgary, our other two sons were returning to Calgary after spending the summer working on a farm in Saskatchewan. As they were nearing Calgary airport, they saw a large plane coming in to land at the airport. They said to each other, "Let's go to the airport and see if Dave is on that plane." To their surprise he was! They were at the right place at the right time. The fourteen-year-old boy was safely home and his two brothers were there to meet him.

The three brothers then went to our friends* place where they were staying and there, Carol, who was preparing to go to the airport, was surprised when Dave and the other two boys walked in. Now all four children were together again.

* Lloyd and Ellen Snyder, former WEC missionaries in Liberia with whom Ron lived while attending the University of Calgary.

Meanwhile at Poko, Hulda and I were eagerly waiting for a letter from Dave to tell us about his flight home after we had said good-bye to him in Isiro. It seemed so long as we waited week after week. The mail only came once a week to Poko. Then one day as we opened B.P. 29* there was Dave's handwriting on a letter. We quickly opened it and read how wonderfully God had answered prayer and that he had made it safely home to Canada, making all the right connections.

* Boite Postale

The remainder of the year was spent in either visiting village churches or teaching students while on the mission station, and winding up the year with the usual Christmas conference.

On March 23, 1973, Hulda and I made a trip to Isiro to apply for a visa for Hulda to return to Canada. There was no problem and the authorities granted it and stamped the seven-month visa in her passport. The purpose for returning to Canada was to attend Carol's graduation from Prairie Bible Institute and to provide a home for Dave over the summer months. Employment for fifteen-year-olds was hard to get and Dave needed money to enroll in grade eleven. Hulda's family was helping to support Dave while we were in Africa.

A week later, I took Hulda to Isiro to catch the plane for Kinshasa and from there home to Canada. Needless to say, my return home to Poko that day was a very lonely three hours. I did not enjoy the thought of returning to an empty house. The Congolese, however, were kind to me. One old man named Ziga would often come around at sunset with his chair and we would sit on the verandah and talk. Others would also come to chat. I asked the pastor to ask a married couple from among the students who didn't have a family, to come and sleep in the dining room of our house so that I wouldn't be alone at nights. Two or three couples agreed to do this and I was grateful for them. Kalama, our faithful house worker, helped me very much in preparing meals and in keeping the house clean. He was on call when I needed him as he lived close by.

During this time, I saw the need of arranging for several village church teachers to meet together in a central church for a week of Bible study and fellowship. It was something like the TEE* work that missions do today. The place chosen to meet was *(a village halfway between Poko and Isiro called)* Nero. The twenty-five village teachers and their wives came and were happy to meet in this way and receive instruction in the Word of God. We had a great time.

Theological Education by Extension

One special meeting I remember, happened in June before school ended. It was with the sixth-grade school children and before they left the mission school to have further education in other schools, I gave them a pep talk on how to know the will of God for their lives and challenged them to make a full commitment of their lives to God and let Him guide them. At the end of June, the school children returned to their villages.

Every week I would look forward to the mail truck's arrival in Poko. Sometimes I would be disappointed if there was nothing, and sometimes excited if I saw a letter from loved ones in Canada or Australia. There was also the usual communication between missionaries and the field director and these letters were much appreciated and encouraging, telling us how God was working in hearts and lives on the other eleven mission stations and areas.

The national church leaders in Ibambi sent an evangelist along with his wife and family to Poko. He was sent to help in a work at Bima, an area south of Poko where there were no missionaries. The church asked me if I could help and take this family from Poko to Bima. I got the truck ready and set out in August. I took one of the students with me to help with the meetings on our return journey.

After we left Poko, we had not gone far when we got caught in a terrific rain storm. I had to drive through a deep hole filled with water and after getting through that the motor spluttered and then stopped. We were in the middle of the road trying to get the motor started. Finally, it started and we drove to a village church and camped for the night. We went on the next day and stayed at a church in Zobia where we had meetings that evening and the next morning. The third day we came to Bima and continued on further to the village where the evangelist was assigned. It was a terrible road with many broken-down bridges. Those people were so happy to have an evangelist and teacher come to live with them.

After a day or so we packed up and started on our homeward journey. We had to tackle this awful road again. This road was hardly used, it was narrow and crossing the bridges was so dangerous, but the Lord protected us and we made it out of the dense forest and back on to a better road. We camped at a village church near a coffee plantation for the night. A large group came to the evening meeting, but I was so exhausted that I couldn't go. The student, Mawa, took the meeting and I spoke the following morning. We visited several churches along the way and preached morning and evening and arrived safely back at Poko.

One day in early October, a letter came from Canada and in it was some good news; Hulda was preparing to return to Poko - and Carol was coming along with her. This gave me something to look forward to.

On October 17, I left Poko early in the morning with the senior pastor and Kalama, the houseboy, to meet Hulda and Carol in Isiro. The plane arrived late in the afternoon and it was so good to see my wife and daughter getting off the plane and coming to meet me. After collecting the baggage, we started on the return trip to Poko. First, we stopped at the local post office in Isiro. I had a letter already written to the three boys in Canada and I wrote a quick postscript saying that their mom and sister had arrived safely, then closed the letter and mailed it.

We arrived back in Poko in the middle of the night and even though most of the folks were asleep, a few light sleepers heard the truck coming up the hill and came to the house to greet their Madame and Carol. At this point and for the next six months, our family was half in Africa and half in Canada.

Carol seemed to remember the Bangala language and was soon able to communicate with the people. One day we moved the piano outside and Carol played for the elementary school children. It was something new for them. Carol taught the students' wives some gymnastics* and took a few classes with the students.

* Aubrey probably meant calisthenics.

It was our 25th wedding anniversary on December 2 and Carol presented us with a scrap book that she had made secretly in her room. This was a pleasant surprise to us and we still have it after being married over 40 years. We had our photo taken, and then in the evening, Carol asked us to sit outside just off the verandah. One by one a line of students formed in front of us and they began to sing. Carol had arranged all this and we certainly had a nice surprise celebration.

On December 7, it was Carol's birthday and it was the first time that she had celebrated her birthday without her twin brother being present.

Following that we received an invitation from Howard and Pam Burns at Malingwia, to come and visit them. We went out west to their station on December 15 and stayed four days with them. They were the family who stayed with us for a while *(in early 1972)* to learn the Bangala language.

When we arrived back at Poko it was time to prepare for the Christmas conference. The Zairian believers pray much about
these conferences and expect God to work. Many souls are saved, backsliders are restored, Christians are encouraged and inspired, and some believers who have been instructed and accepted by the church are baptized. They receive the right hand of fellowship from the elders and now can take part in the communion service, as members of the church. After a meal all together the fifteen to eighteen hundred people return

168

to their villages while the pastors, evangelists and catechists (*unpaid teachers and voluntary workers*) stay for church business meetings.

In January of 1974, we drove down to Ibambi to attend a field council meeting. Delegates came from the various mission stations and met with the field director and two or three missionaries who had been elected to the field council.

While we were in this part of the world, Carol had the opportunity to fly to Nyankunde, a medical center in north-east Zaire. A doctor who was visiting the nearby hospital at Nebobongo was returning and Carol was invited to go along and visit the much larger hospital and medical work at Nyankunde. After four days, she returned on the MAF plane to Nebobongo where she stayed for three weeks helping and observing. Hulda and I returned to Poko and Carol came later with one of the nurses.

During the field council meetings in January, we were asked if we could move from Poko and go south 400 miles where there was a great need. The missionaries who had opened up this work at Mulita station* were home on furlough and they had been chosen to be the new field leaders to take the place of Mr. Scholes who had recently died at Ibambi. The Graingers would be thus be moving from Mulita to Ibambi. There was also a nurse who would be soon returning to Mulita from furlough and the mission didn't want her to be alone. In addition, there was a small Bible school there that needed teachers and we could both teach and meet that need.

* *Jim and Ida Grainger*

Hulda and I didn't want to leave the work at Poko, nor did the people want us to leave. After prayer and seeking guidance though, we felt we should obey those over us in the Lord, and go to the regions beyond. We were thankful that Carol was with us and could help us move. She obtained an extension on her visa allowing her to stay a little longer.

We thought it was advisable for us to sell the piano as the road to Mulita was terrible beyond description, so we started looking for a buyer. A missionary family in Isiro was interested and they ended up buying it.

We started packing and by the end of April we were ready to leave. The mission truck came from Ibambi to load up and haul our things. On the Sunday, I remember preaching my farewell sermon in the Poko church and on Monday morning we said goodbye to our faithful friends, fellow workers and students at Poko. We travelled with the larger mission truck in our smaller Chev pick-up to Ibambi where we spent a day or two. Then on to Wamba, and the day following, we camped at Niania where Pastor Idoti was working.

From there we journeyed to Kisangani to buy provisions, gas* and kerosene.* We needed these things as there were no stores at Mulita, since it is a very isolated place, even further south than Opienge. We left Kisangani late in the afternoon and stayed the night at a village church. Things there were very primitive. The following day we arrived at the mission station in Lubutu where there were no missionaries there at that time. We stayed the night and then as the road that ran directly from Lubutu to Mulita was impassable, we had to go the long way around which took us two days of travelling instead of one day.

* Fuel for the truck was bought in 45-gallon drums and smaller drums of kerosene were for the fridge and lanterns.

From Lubutu we first travelled east then south. We came to a village near evening and saw a government rest house, so we stopped but found it was occupied by a Zairian government official. He agreed for us to sleep in the cook house at the back which we did. We were so tired after not only having to change a flat tire on our truck, but also having to help push the big truck when it got stuck in the mud. What made things worse that night was the nearby villagers beating drums and dancing all night long. One bright spot in that dark evening was that we met some students from the Mulita Bible school who were trekking and preaching in the area where we camped. They were so happy to see us and brought us firewood and some food.

The next day we journeyed on, crossing two large rivers and arriving first at Punia and then Mulita towards evening, weary and tired. We unloaded the mission truck and our pickup truck, and moved everything into the empty house. Later the mission chauffeur left to take the truck back to Ibambi, and the three of us were alone amongst strangers.

Soon the Bible School students returned from trekking to begin another term. The leader of the school brought the students to our door one day to welcome us and they sang a hymn for us in Kiswahili, *Am I a soldier of the cross, a follower of the lamb?*

We had to change our language now and speak in Swahili instead of Bangala. Courses were studied and soon we were ready to teach. We taught classes in the mornings from 6:30 am until noon and spent the afternoons preparing for the next day. Some Sundays we visited the leper camp nearby and shared the gospel with them. Some of the lepers were keen Christians, living in hope that one day their diseased bodies would be exchanged for a new body, when they passed away out of this life here on earth.

We didn't see many white people at Mulita. In the year we were there, we made one trip back to Kisangani to buy provisions and gas. We also purchased two bicycles; one for a pastor to help him visit village churches. There were fifty-six churches in the area and only four pastors.

One day the nurse who had been on furlough returned to Mulita from England. Isabel came riding a bicycle onto the station. The weekly plane from Kisangani had brought her to Punia, where she then hired some porters to carry her baggage, and a teacher lent her his bicycle to travel the several miles out to Mulita. We hadn't had any news of her coming, but were very happy to have her living next door and sharing in the work.

An interesting side note, lest one think there are no more missionaries in Congo, that medical, educational or church work has ceased, or that the places in Aubrey's story are just historical towns - here is a link to a Belfast Telegraph story from January 2015. WEC missionary Maud Kells went to Mulita after Isabel left, and the 75-year-old nurse-midwife was shot by bandits during a break-in and had to be airlifted by MAF to Nebobongo first, then to Nyankunde.

According to a story in the Belfast Telegraph, on January 10, 2019, she was returning for one last time at the age of 79 to deliver medical supplies to Mulita - link available via the blog.

It was interesting to hear fifteen years later, that three couples whom we had taught at the Mulita Bible School were now ordained pastors and still in the ministry. Others that we had taught at Poko were still laboring for God as pastors and evangelists and one couple became teachers at the new Poko Bible School.

In June it was time to take Carol to the Kisangani airport to return home to Canada via England, after having stayed with us for eight months. Ken had found her a job in Banff for the summer.

Then July 6 came and that was the date for the wedding of Ron to Myra Elliott in Three Hills, Alberta. We couldn't attend because we were so far away, but we had sent a cassette tape home with Carol to express our happiness for them. Later we received a tape of the wedding ceremony.

On October 9 a man came to our door carrying a sack of mail. We received thirty-four letters that day as our mail had been held up somewhere for five months. I remember the date because on this day my blood pressure was 178 over 120. For several months I hadn't been feeling well, even though I was taking pills for blood pressure which a doctor prescribed for me. And though I carried on, I didn't know for how much longer.

It must have been about this time that Isabel told Hulda that she had better get her husband home or she would be losing him.

So, I wrote to Jim Grainger, the field director, to see if he would be interested in buying our truck or if he knew of someone who might be interested. I also told him I couldn't carry on much longer as I was getting weaker. He replied favourably and said he would buy our truck and told us he would come down to see us after Christmas. We prepared for the conference and it was a time of meeting with the Christians from the fifty-six churches in this area. I preached at one of the meetings.

Early in 1975, we prepared to return to Australia mainly because of health problems. We had a sale and were able to sell most of our belongings which allowed us to purchase our tickets to fly to Melbourne, Australia. Two of the pastors took charge of the Bible School. Another missionary brought the field director down to Mulita in March to take possession of our Chev truck and to take us to Kisangani to catch the plane to Kinshasa.

We stayed with friends in Kinshasa and then purchased tickets to South Africa. In Kinshasa, I was told I didn't need a visa for South Africa, but I found that was false later when they wouldn't let me out of the airport at Johannesburg. So, we slept at the airport and the next morning I obtained a visa. We then phoned some friends and they met us and took us to their home. When we went to the airport again to proceed on our journey, Hulda was not allowed on the plane because they said she needed a visa to enter Australia. Our kind friends took us to Pretoria by bus and at the Australian embassy, Hulda was given a visa for six months to live in Australia. The following day we left South Africa and came down on the island of Mauritius to refuel. We crossed the Indian Ocean and arrived at Perth in West Australia. We were met there by our mission friends and stayed there a couple of days. I phoned my brother Rupert in Bendigo, and asked him to arrange for someone to meet us in Melbourne. When we arrived in Melbourne in mid-March, my sister Gladys, was there to meet us along with the Woods and Lorna Falls. We travelled together in two cars as far as the Wood's place in Castlemaine, then Lorna brought us to Rupert and Evelyn's home in Bendigo. Eventually Gladys took us to live with her in her home where we stayed several months.

April 5 was Ken and Teresa's wedding day in Arizona, USA. We phoned them from Bendigo and wished them well. It was so good to hear their voices after being separated from them for three and a half years.

During this time in Australia we were praying much about our future and seeking the Lord's will and mind for the next step in our lives. We attended a mission conference in Sydney and requested prayer for our future. One of the leaders there said to us as we talked about our future, "If your children want you, go to them; ours don't".

We felt the Lord was guiding us to Canada.

Chapter 10

Retirement In Canada
1975 to 1989

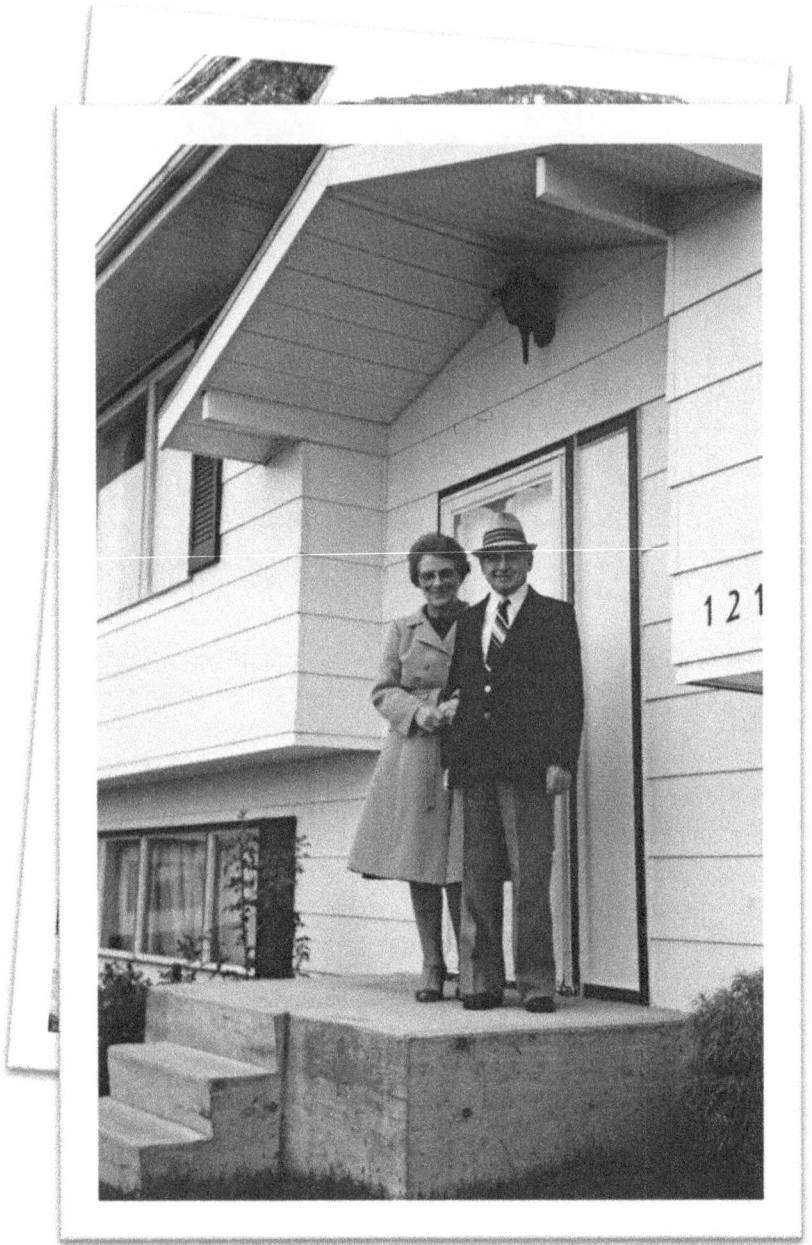

HULDA AND AUBREY ON THE FRONT STEPS OF THEIR HOME IN THREE
HILLS, 1982

1975 to 1989

1975

After we had been in Australia for three months we decided to settle in Canada where our children were and so in June, Hulda left for Canada to attend Dave's graduation from High School on June 11. I was booked up with meetings until the end of July, but when those were done, I left for Canada as well.

When Ron heard of our plans to return to Canada, he looked for a house for us to rent and found one on Centre Street North in Calgary. This became home for us until the end of the year. Carol and Dave came to live with us. Ken worked in a garage a few blocks away and he and Teresa had a suite not too far away. Ron and Myra lived in Regina where Ron was studying at the seminary of Canadian Bible College.

Carol had set her date for October 11 to be married to Jim Elliott and we now focused on preparing for our daughter's wedding; Hulda was busy making the wedding dresses for Carol and the three bridesmaids. I helped by mailing out the wedding invitations.

Carol and Jim were married in the Foothills Alliance Church with the reception held in the basement of the church building. Ken was the emcee and during the program, refreshments were handed around to the guests.

During November, Hulda and I went job hunting.* We drove from Calgary to Swift Current, then on to Regina to visit Ron and Myra. From there we went on to Steinbach in Manitoba to visit Hulda's two brothers - Henry and Elaine, Pete and Anne. On our way back, we stopped in at Shilo to visit another brother and his wife, Abe and Lydia.

A job was necessary for Aubrey, as being an Australian citizen with only landed immigrant status in Canada, he had to be employed here for two full years in a row to qualify for Canadian pension

From there, it was back to Regina, where we heard news of an opening for a couple to work at the Dalmeny Home for the Aged. This was a senior citizens care facility near Saskatoon, Saskatchewan. We made contact with them and two members came to see us when we returned to Calgary. One cold day in December, we went to Dalmeny to meet with the Board members and visit the home. We accepted this job and returned to Calgary to pack up. Before leaving we were able to celebrate Christmas; after being away for four years, it was so nice to be with all the family and we had a great time together.

1976

On January 6 of the new year, we moved to Dalmeny to begin work in the Home for the Aged. Dave decided to move with us to Saskatchewan and helped us move. He loaded both cars, drove his car and we followed in our car. A room in the Home near the office was ready for us and a small room was prepared for Dave. Dave found work at a flour mill in Saskatoon and drove the twenty minutes to work there every morning.

Hulda was Matron and Director of Care for the Home and I worked in the office as Secretary and Treasurer. I also led both morning devotions before breakfast, and evening devotions after supper.

There were thirty guests living in the Home that year. I prayed and gave thanks for the good meals provided and dismissed the folks when everyone finished their meal.

A staff of fifteen workers came each day to work at the Home. Every morning I would walk downtown to pick up the mail at the local post office and when I returned would distribute letters to the guests in their rooms.

My job at the end of each month was to collect money from the guests and take it to Saskatoon and deposit it in a bank. Then I would write out cheques for the staff workers and keep record of that. When we had board meetings I had to take down the minutes and later send a copy to each board member. I arranged speakers to come to the Home to hold a morning service for the guests at 10 am. Some of the guests were able to worship in the local churches. We would start work each day at 7 am and work until 3 pm, and as we were living in the Home, we were always on call.

We heard of a house lot for sale in the town and went to see it. We contacted the owner and decided to buy it, then soon the house was built on that lot and were able to move into it at the end of 1976. The pastor of the Dalmeny Bible Church along with staff and friends came and surprised us with a hearty house warming. During this first year at the Home I became a Senior Citizen.

During the year of 1976, there were three couples* in Hulda's family who had been married for 25 years and they decided to celebrate their wedding anniversaries together near Saskatoon at a place called Pike Lake. It was a wonderful summer weekend at the lake for the Schroeder family.

*Laura and Clarence, Abe and Lydia, Jake and Margaret

On November 15, our first grandchild was born in Regina to Carol and Jim.* Her name was Julie Dawn Elliott and Hulda and I drove to Regina to see Carol and Jim and their new baby. Hulda stayed on for a few days and I came back to be on duty Monday morning.

*Carol and Jim had moved to Regina for Jim to study at the seminary of CMA's Canadian Bible College and Seminary. Both Ron and Myra and Jim and Carol followed the same path to Africa - a two-year masters program at the Seminary, a two or three year term pastoring a church, a year of French study in Albertville, France, and then finally to the country where they would be working - Zaire for the former, Guinea for the latter.

1977

I didn't retire at the age of 65 but continued on working through the year of 1977. In October, Dave decided to take a six-month trip to Zaire. He had this in his mind for some time and had earned enough money at the flour mill to pay for his ticket to Africa. He enjoyed helping at the medical center at Nebobongo and at Ibambi. Then he went to Poko to visit friends and was there for the Christmas conference during which time he was baptized. On his return, he visited England and arrived safely back in Dalmeny on March 16, 1978.

1978

I quit work early in 1978. It was time to retire. Although Hulda continued to work, we put our house up for sale and waited several months until it was sold.

During June and July there were three deaths in our families. My brother, Rupert, died on June 22nd at the age of 62. He had a heart attack and passed into the presence of the Lord a few hours later.

Hulda's brother Henry Schroeder, who was the pastor at Steinbach Alliance Church, died of cancer on July 21. Ron and Myra, who were pastoring a church in Vegreville, Alberta, stopped in to pick us up in Dalmeny, Saskatchewan and together we went to the funeral in Manitoba.

When we returned from the funeral to Dalmeny, we were having our evening meal when the phone rang. It was a call from Australia saying that my sister had died on July 27 and was now in the presence of the Lord. This was just over a month after my brother had passed away. I felt that I should go to her funeral as I was now the only one left in our immediate family. Ron took me to a travel agent in Saskatoon where I booked my flight to Melbourne. I left the following day and my nephew Rodney met me at the airport in Melbourne.*

Gladys never married and Rupert and Evelyn had one child, Rodney. He is our only Brown cousin - it is unfortunate that we live half a world away from each other.

I arrived in time for the funeral of Gladys and stayed with Evelyn and Rodney. There was a lot of work to do at the home where Gladys lived and I had to take care of many things. I brought back to Canada a few things such as old family photos and a box of letters that my mother had saved, dating back as far as 1938. As we read these letters later they brought back memories of incidents that I had long forgotten. I spent a month in Australia visiting relatives and friends. WEC friends came to Sydney airport to see me off on my return to Canada.

On October 8, our first grandson was born in Three Hills. God gave Ken and Teresa a baby boy; they named him Jeremy. Children are a heritage from the Lord. Then on December 22, our second grandson was born. Carol and Jim had a baby boy at Barrhead, Alberta, where they were now pastoring a church. They named this baby, James Aubrey.

1979

Our house was sold in Dalmeny and preparations were made to move. It wasn't a sudden move. We had plenty of time to think and pray about where we should go for our retirement. The Lord indicated Three Hills. Ken and Teresa were living in Three Hills at that time as Ken had a job working in a garage in town.

We made arrangements with the WEC representative in Three Hills to live in the WEC Home, one mile north of town, while we looked for a house or lot. Ron, Jim and Ken all came to Dalmeny and helped us move to Three Hills. After looking at several houses which were up for sale we decided to buy a lot on the eastern side of town that already had a basement built on the lot. We then ordered a package from Nelson Homes to fit on this basement and had it delivered. Stan Christon, a missionary friend helped us build the house and we moved into it in November 3. We were happy to have good neighbors and a quiet location in which to retire.

We had a line installed through the telephone system from Prairie Bible Institute and could then tune in and listen to chapel and Sunday services as well as the annual conferences. Later we could listen to the Moody Network.

We became members of Prairie Tabernacle Congregation and served for six years with the visitation teams. We visited a lot of people in their homes and others were invited to our home for a meal. We were happy to minister in this way; the blessings were mutual. I joined the senior men's prayer group which met at 9 am every Wednesday morning. It started soon after we came here and still continues, nearly ten years now.

On September 10, Ron and Myra left for Albertville, France, to do a year of French language study before going out to Zaire for their first term with the Christian and Missionary Alliance. We met as a family - all twelve of us, in the WEC Home for five days together before they left. That was great!

It seemed appropriate that as Aubrey and Hulda ended their active missionary career and began their retirement in Three Hills, the oldest of their children was now beginning his career in Africa.

On January 31st, we had a pleasant surprise. Twenty-seven folks came to the door of our new house for a house-warming party. We welcomed them and managed to find a place for everyone as they squeezed into the front room. We enjoyed the evening as we got to know different people from the church and the town. The pastor led in devotions. Ken acted the part of emcee. This was not a surprise to him nor the other children with us!

According to our guest book the first two visitors we had in the year of 1980 were two young men from Ethiopia who were students at PBI. The total number of visitors for this first year in Three Hills was 57; some were here just for a meal and a visit, while others stayed a night or for a few days.

During this first year we had a few loads of top soil brought in the back of our lot to make a garden and by the month of May it was ready to start putting in our garden. I have always enjoyed gardening and watching things grow. Man plants the seeds and God sends the rain and sunshine and gives the increase.

I read in a newspaper that here in Alberta one has approximately one hundred and fifty days or five months from the last frost to the first frost in fall to plant a garden and to bring the vegetables inside the house and store them in a cold room.

During the summer months Jim and Carol with Julie and Jamie stayed here with us. On September 5 we said goodbye to them as they left for Albertville, France, for a year of language study before going on to Guinea, West Africa, to teach in a Bible School. Meanwhile Ron and Myra had finished their French language study and went to Maduda in Zaire to start learning the Kikongo language.

During these years in Three Hills I had more time to spend in reading the Bible and taking time in prayer each morning interceding for the advance of the gospel, holding the ropes of those whom I knew personally and for others whom I had read or heard about. This took my thoughts and prayers to many countries where God's servants are labouring. The prayer list seemed to get longer and longer over the years. New missionary candidates were going to the fields from Prairie Tabernacle Congregation and they would challenge us older people to pray for them. Prayer letters would come to keep us informed of their needs and activities. It was certainly not hard to pray without ceasing.

I enjoyed reading good and meaningful books which edified. I also found time to read the missionary magazines, some fifteen or so, that came to our mail box each month.

One thing we looked forward to year by year was attending the two missionary conferences held at PBI. The spring conference and graduation were combined and generally held around Easter time. The fall conference was held usually in October and the emphasis was more on Deeper Life teaching. Many mission representatives would attend these conferences and be ready to help the students and others to get to know other needy parts of the world where people were still waiting for someone to come and tell them about Jesus. Several would speak about their mission during conference days. There would be five meetings a day.

1981

On March 22 our third grandson was born here in Three Hills. Ken and Teresa named him Jason. During the summer months Ken and Teresa put their house up for sale and it was sold in a few days. This was in preparation for them to go to Albertville, France, to study French. Their goal was to do missionary work in Zaire with the Africa Inland Mission. On arriving in Albertville, they were happy to spend a little time with Jim and Carol* before they left for Africa.
*who had just finished studying at the same school

1982

I can't remember very much of what took place during the year of 1982 apart from writing letters to the children and going to the post office five days a week hoping to bring home a letter from loved ones overseas. After breakfast each morning Hulda and I would read Scripture and read the Daily Bread notes. We have read these notes for many years and reading that has been a blessing to us. This year three families were overseas and we made time to remember each one and their needs before the Lord. We would commit them all to His care and keeping. Their time in Africa was eight hours ahead of our time and their day would be nearly over when we were starting our day here.

After supper we would have our evening devotions and at that time we would pray for those on our prayer list. On Monday evening we would pray for Africa and several missionaries and national workers whom we knew were serving the Lord on that continent. Tuesday was Europe, Wednesday was Asia, Thursday was South America, Friday was North America and Saturday was Australia. On Sunday we would pray for our relatives and nieces and nephews.

A book I used in my private devotions was Operation World* which was helpful in giving information and needs for prayer for countries around the world. "God so loved the world," John 3:16. More things are wrought by prayer than this world could ever know. Psalm 5:3 says, "My voice shalt Thou hear in the morning, 0 Lord; in the morning will I direct my prayer unto Thee, and I will look up.

*Operation World by Patrick Johnstone originally, and continued by Jason Mandryk, both from WEC International.

On September 21, Hulda and I went by bus to Twin Falls in Idaho, USA to visit Hulda's sister Emma, for two weeks. It was a nice restful holiday for us.

Later in the year Dave, with his friend Arnie Friesen, went overseas to visit the Cook Islands, New Zealand, and Australia. They worked for a time on a sheep farm in New Zealand and in Australia they visited some of the Brown tives. They spent Christmas in Tasmania, and before returning to Canada they worked on a dairy farm in New South Wales.

1983

Early in the year Jim and Carol with their two children planned to fly to France from Guinea to have their third child. Hulda started making preparations and a booking to go to Lyon, France, to help with the family while Carol was in hospital. Hulda's flight took her to London on February 27 where she stayed at the WEC headquarters at Bulstrode and from there across to France. A baby girl was born on March 2 and was named Jacquelyn Elisabeth.

I well remember that day of March 2 because I received two very exciting phone calls. One was from Jim in France announcing the birth of a new granddaughter and the other a few hours later from Vancouver. It was Dave on the phone saying he and his friend had arrived back in Canada from their

Australian trip; after a day or so Dave was home in Three Hills. It was great to see him and have his company while Hulda was still in France. It was delightful to me to hear news of loved ones from Dave, and also the various places he visited which were so familiar to me. One was the place where I grew up.

After a while Hulda returned and gave us the news of the happenings in France and her brief stay in England on her way home.

In July, Ron and Myra came home on furlough from Zaire after being away from Canada for four years. After a period of rest, they were assigned to visiting Alliance churches here in Alberta. Ron would be at one church while Myra was scheduled to be at another church in the vicinity. Sometimes they were together for a meeting. One church gave them a nice shower of groceries which they greatly appreciated.

One day we drove up to Camrose to meet Ron and Myra. They were still on tour taking meetings. The occasion was Ron's birthday. We celebrated over a noon meal or October 27th. Then we visited for a while, gave them their mail and then drove home. When we arrived home the cement floor had been laid for our new double garage. It was a very cold night and a tarpaulin was over the cement and a motor working, to pump hot air under the tarpaulin to keep the cement from freezing. It worked and no damage was done.

The garage was finished before Christmas and we were so thankful for it and that our car did not have to be outside during the winter months. The garage was not only for cars but was used for a storage place for members of the family when they left for missionary work overseas.

On December 19 Ron and Myra's first child was born. They called her Bethany Marie. Then came Christmas and it was time to celebrate the Savior's birth.

1984

At the beginning of the year, at our house at 1211 - 1st Street North in Three Hills, there was a baby shower for Bethany Marie Brown. Twenty-five ladies attended for the happy occasion.

During our years in Three Hills, first from 1966 to 1971 and later from 1979 to 1984 we were privileged and blessed through the ministry of the founder and president of Prairie Bible Institute. We listened many times, as we were able, to his lectures to the students by way of campus line. Nearly every Sunday morning during our first stay in Three Hills, Rev. L. E. Maxwell would preach. In 1984 the Lord called him home. We attended the large funeral conducted by his friend Rev. Stephen Olford on February 11. Rev. Maxwell had lived in Three Hills from 1922 to 1984. I for one, was grateful to God that I had shaken hands on several occasions with this man and had listened and heard God speaking through this gifted preacher and teacher.

We were happy to welcome home Jim and Carol and their three children from Guinea after four years. We met them at the Calgary airport on June 8.

Early in the next month of July, Hulda and I went with Jim and Carol and family to Swan River, Manitoba. The occasion was to attend the wedding of Dave to Dianne Jersak. We stayed at Rosetown in Saskatchewan the first night, and the following day made it to Swan River. It was nice meeting Dianne's family at that time. Ron and Myra were still around then, and he married them on July 7. That was the last wedding of our four children. Our home seemed a bit empty. After the wedding ceremony, a large group of invited guests gathered in the basement of the church at Minitonas for a delicious meal and a program where Dave and Dianne's friend was the emcee.

A couple of weeks after this wedding, Ron and Myra with Bethany left for their second term in Zaire. The good-byes don't get any easier as the years roll by. The crates Ron packed in our garage were shipped off soon after they left and arrived safely in Zaire.

Carol and Jim lived in a house a short distance away from us in Three Hills. During the furlough year, Jim was often away on meetings. Julie and Jamie attended Prairie Elementary School which wasn't far away. Carol was able to be with Jim at some of his meetings and sometimes went alone to speak at ladies' meetings.

Some of the folks who visited us in 1984 came from Nigeria, Liberia, Zaire, Gambia, Kenya, Guinea, Pakistan, and India.

1985

Towards the middle of 1985, a phone call came from Toronto. It was Ken giving us the time of their arrival at the Calgary airport. We got things ready at our house and were delighted to welcome them home on the second of June. They had been away four years serving the Lord at the Nyankunde Medical Centre in north-east Zaire. Before they left, they visited the area where Hulda and I had previously worked at Poko and Nala in the Uele district of Zaire.

Ken, Teresa, and their two boys, Jeremy and Jason, lived with us until they found a house to buy here in Three Hills. They decided to buy a house on 2nd Avenue North and we were surprised that it was the same house that was our home from 1967 to 1971. Ken got a job in a garage nearby.

At the end of June, there was a 25th wedding anniversary in the family and as it was nearby it brought many relatives to Alberta. One day we had seven families for dinner besides our own children.

Then in August there was a 40th anniversary celebration of Hulda's brother Art and his wife, Violet, in Cranbrook, British Columbia. This was another large reunion for Hulda's family.

Dave and Dianne moved to Alberta from Winnipeg during the summer of 1985 and bought a duplex in the north part of Calgary. Dianne worked at the Foothills Hospital as a lab technologist in the microbiology department and Dave started a two-year program in Photojournalism at SAIT.*

*Southern Alberta Institute of Technology (other SAIT alumni from our family were Ken (Automotive Mechanics), Myra (Journalism) and Jim (Electrical).

Meanwhile Jim and Carol with their three children were assigned by the Christian and Missionary Alliance to work in Quebec for three years. They bought a house in Quebec City which was central for their work. Jim and another pastor were doing TEE work. They had classes in Montreal, Quebec City, and further east at Rimouski. Julie and Jamie attended a Christian school quite close to where they lived and had a great opportunity to learn the French language, although it must have been difficult for them when they started school there. Jim and Carol were also involved in a French speaking church quite a distance away.

On August 16, I had the great joy of meeting my cousin, Mildred Hulme, from Australia. We had a few hours together over a meal at the Calgary airport. Dave and Dianne accompanied Hulda and I that evening. Mildred had been staying for a while with her daughter and her husband in Portugal; they were employed there. Now they were all returning home to Australia via England and Canada. It was so nice to meet them after not seeing each other for many years.

We enjoyed having Ken and Teresa and the two boys so close here in Three Hills. When we needed them they were there to help. Jeremy and Jason had a little sister come to live with them in December when Jodilynn Denae was born on December the first, just across the road from our house in the new Three Hills Hospital.

The twelve books I read during 1985 were these:

Perhaps Today: The Rapture of the Church – H. Vander Lugt
The Blood of the Cross - Andrew Murray
The Best Half of Life – Raymond C. Ortland
How To Say No To A Stubborn Habit - Erwin Lutzer
But God - A. B. Simpson
The Winds of God - Raymond Davis
Dare to Discipline - James Dobson
Approaching Hoofbeats - Billy Graham
Good Marriages Take Time - David and Carole Hocking
Here We Stand - Stewart Dinnen
Growing Strong In The Seasons Of Life - Charles Swindoll
Every Day With Jesus - George Duncan

1986

As the new year started things went on as usual. When winter was over, the month of May came along and it was time to plant potatoes, vegetables and flowers. The lawn had to be raked and then cut once a week in the springtime.

In June, I was excited to have a visit from my Uncle Charlie from Australia. Mr. Charles Wood and his wife Joyce, arrived at the Calgary airport on the 19th. He found it difficult to walk and used a wheelchair to get around. They had left Australia a few months before and had spent time in England

and Scotland visiting relatives and friends. On their return journey, they decided to visit us here in Three Hills. We had such a happy time together. We talked over old times as I knew Uncle Charlie when I was a boy and I asked many questions about my relatives and friends in Australia. Uncle Charlie was a man who loved the Lord, a preacher of the Gospel for over sixty years. He went into the public schools and taught religious instruction every week, reaching hundreds of children. He encouraged me in my early Christian life, and stood behind me when I left for the mission field. He supported me and my wife and children with daily prayers and sent financial help from time to time. One evening we took the Woods to a concert in Calgary where Dave was performing and they so enjoyed that.

The day before they left us to return to Australia, Hulda made and decorated a birthday cake for him as he would soon be ninety years old. After he returned to Australia, he went home to be with the Lord just before his ninety-first birthday.

Ken came over in July and built a fence at the back of our property to make things more private. I painted the fence later. In September it was time to pick beans, and after the onions had dried, we brought them into the basement. We dug out the potatoes and brought them in and stored them away in a cold room. The first frost came early that month. In October the leaves turn such a beautiful color; later on they fall to the ground or get blown away with the wind. These months are called "fall" in this part of the world. People put snow tires on their cars in preparation for winter.

On November 10, Hulda and I left Calgary by bus bound for Quebec to visit Carol and Jim and their three children. Neither of us had been in eastern Canada before. It was a long way and took us three days and two nights riding on the bus. We had one stopover in Swift Current, visiting a relative there.

Jim, Carol, and children met us in Montreal and after some sightseeing, and a meal, they drove us to their home in Quebec City, which is the capital of the province of Quebec. We soon realized that while we were still in Canada, we were in a different culture, with a different language. We enjoyed our three weeks in Quebec City and did some sightseeing in the older part of the city. We visited the school and met the teachers of Julie and Jamie. We attended the church services at Levis, where Jim led the choir and Carol taught a Sunday School class in French. Sometimes Jim would preach in this church. The first Sunday I didn't understand much of the sermon as the preacher spoke very fast. However the next Sunday another man preached and I could hear almost everything he said. Carol was the organist at this church.

Quebec had lots of snow that year and in some places the snow was piled up eight to ten feet high in front of the houses. One sight that was unusual to us was that along both sides of the streets in the residential areas, people had built makeshift garages of plywood in the driveways, right out near the curb. This of course saved them from shoveling snow in the winter time. When winter was over the garages were dismantled and put away for the next winter.

For our return trip to Calgary we decided to take the train. We had two stopovers visiting relatives and that was very enjoyable. Dave and Dianne met us at the train station in Calgary and brought us back to Three Hills on first of December. We did our Christmas mail and prepared for Christmas and New Year.

1987

In January, I thought it was time to start writing my memoirs. Ron had sent me an outline and encouraged me to get going. I wasn't getting any younger and getting more forgetful as the years went by. One day I took our car across to the car wash to have it cleaned up. After it had been through the wash, I parked it in the sun alongside other cars to dry. Then I went for a short walk. On returning I started polishing it and it looked like new. I went to get into the car and realized it belonged to somebody else - it wasn't ours. So I had to start all over again and polish the right car.

Ron and Myra returned to Canada during this year for a short time. Their second daughter was born and they called her Rebecca Jane.

Jim and Carol came over from Quebec during the summer. At Prairie Bible Institute they had a big celebration which they called "Homecoming". Hundreds of the alumni came here to Three Hills for the weekend of July 23 to 26. It was well organized and a time of spiritual refreshing and enjoyment for all. Many came to the event from different parts of the world where they had been serving the Lord.

A few days later the Town of Three Hills celebrated their 75th anniversary and there was a second homecoming. Many old timers who had moved away from Three Hills came back to celebrate and meet with friends.

During the summer we went to Kelowna, BC, to attend the 40th wedding anniversary of Hulda's sister Luella and her husband Ted Epp. It so happened that all of our children with their families could come to Kelowna for that weekend. For the past eight years we were not able for all of us to be together. This was a very memorable occasion. On our way back from Kelowna we stopped in Calgary and had a family photo taken.

On September 14 our fourth grandson was born; Ken and Teresa named him Justin Robert. All of their four children were born here in Three Hills.

During the latter part of 1987, Ken and Teresa were making preparations to return to Africa. It was a busy time for them, selling their house, packing up, storing things, making bookings and farewells. They left on November 18 and after a few days in Kenya flew over the ocean to join the African Inland Mission team in the Comoro Islands.

Dave and Dianne invited us to come and spend Christmas with them in Calgary which we enjoyed and have happy memories of that time together.

1988

There were seven highlights of the year which I want to write about.

First was the Winter Olympic Games held in Calgary eighty-five miles away from where we lived. People came from many countries to take part in and to watch the events which began on February 13. On television we watched the torch being carried each day from the east coast of Canada to western Canada and finally saw it passing through the streets of Calgary and right into the stadium to light the flame there. This was something I will never forget. I enjoyed watching on television as the athletes from the different countries marched into the arena carrying their country's flag at the opening ceremonies.

191

On March 15, Hulda and I left Calgary for two weeks to visit Jim, Carol and family in Quebec. This time we had heard about a seat sale and made bookings with Air Canada. Jim, Carol and Jacquelyn met us at the Quebec City airport; the older two children were in school. We left Calgary at ten after one in the morning and it took three hours to get to Toronto and from there on to Quebec City arriving at 11 am their time. During our stay in Quebec, Jim took us to see the maple trees and how they extract the syrup from the trees and then send it to the factory where it is processed for sale. We bought a few jars to bring back home with us.

On June 12, twelve ladies from around Three Hills came here to our home to honor Hulda and celebrate her seventieth birthday. One of the neighbors made the birthday cake. It was supposed to be a surprise but it didn't quite turn out that way. However, Hulda received many nice cards and good wishes and she enjoyed the happy occasion when our own children were far from home at that time. The names of the guests who attended are in the records of our guest book. Carol had written out the invitations to the ladies which she sent to me to deliver.

I had a very welcome visitor come to see me in June from Australia. I had met Ken Booth fifty years ago before I left for the mission field early in 1938. Ken had graduated from Melbourne Bible Institute and later went to India as a missionary. After having spent many years in India and becoming the field director there, he was asked to take over the leadership of the mission in Australia. He was in Eastern Canada for a conference and he phoned someone he knew in Alberta and wanted to arrange a time when he could come and visit us. The date was fixed for June 15 and we had the joy of meeting Ken again and having him stay overnight in our home.

Aubrey was also thrilled to welcome his cousin's daughter and her husband, Lorna and Lindsay Falls, who also visited Three Hills during the summer. They farmed not too far from where Aubrey grew up.

Three days after this visit, Hulda and Dave drove to Saskatoon, Saskatchewan, to meet up with Jim and Carol and bring their three children to Three Hills while Jim and Carol attended the Assembly meetings of the C&MA for a week. After that they joined their family in Three Hills for the summer holidays. Their three-year term in Quebec was completed, and

now they were assigned to Cote d'Ivoire *(Ivory Coast)* in Africa. They were busy getting ready to move to a place called
Yamoussoukro to teach in a Bible School there. We said goodbye to them as they left us on August 3.

During the months of October and November, Dave and
Dianne came to live with us. They were making preparations
to do a short term with a mission in Zimbabwe. While here in
Three Hills, they painted our living room, hallway and dining
room, and did many other things for us.

As our 40th wedding anniversary was approaching, early
in December they arranged for us to have a portrait
en. Then they prepared an anniversary meal for us on December 2nd and before dessert was served, the doorbell rang. Unknown to us, three couples had been invited to share the rest
of the evening with us. After singing and having dessert and
coffee, Dave had prepared and presented an interesting slide
presentation of things that had happened during our forty
years of married life. There were some musical items and a
phone call from Australia congratulating us from a relative
there.

After a long wait, finally word came from Zimbabwe that
a work permit had been granted to work at the mission hospital in Karanda, and so Dave and Dianne left for Africa on December 14. They first spent a few weeks with Ron and Myra in
Zaire over the Christmas and New Year season and arrived in
Zimbabwe on January 15.

As none of our children could be home for Christmas that
year, we accepted an invitation from Hulda's sister, Emma, to
spend Christmas with her in Twin Falls. We left Calgary by
bus on December 19 and travelled the 800 miles south to Idaho, USA. We really enjoyed the two weeks we spent
there. When we arrived home, there was a huge box of mail
waiting for us and lots of snow around.

1989

The last year of the eighties ended with a ten-day visit in May
to relatives living in Abbotsford, British Columbia. It was
great to see once again God's handiwork as we travelled by
bus through the Rocky Mountains.

On returning home we received a phone call from an Australian relative *(Wayne Brown)* who was visiting friends in Cal-

193

gary. We made arrangements to bring him out to Three Hills for a meal. It was a short visit, but during those few hours with him we got caught up on news of relatives and friends from "down under".

During June and July of 1989, we made two trips to Calgary airport to meet and bring home two of our children and their families returning from mission fields in Africa. It was good to see them all again after being absent from each other for a time.

Later on in the year, Hulda and I were able to go east to Saskatchewan to see Hulda's brother, Jake, who was ill in Main Centre. We were also able to visit with our son Ron and his wife and family who were back for a time at the Alliance college, as well as other relatives in Regina.

The Christmas of 1989 was special as there were twelve of us together, six adults and six children. Other members of the family were absent being overseas.

Some Lessons I Have Learned In Life

The fifth of the ten commandments in the Bible reads thus from Exodus 20:12, "Honor thy father and thy mother that thy days may be long upon the land which the Lord thy God giveth thee." This was one of the first lessons I learned in life, to obey my parents. I loved them and honoured them. They were strict; when disobedient I was punished.

During school years I learnt to be punctual, otherwise there was a penalty. I learned in the classroom that it was better to listen and obey the teacher than to ignore what was said. I also learned not to talk to my friends in class. After writing out "I must not talk in school" one hundred times after school was dismissed, it got through to me that I had better smarten up and keep the rules. Another time I had to write a hundred lines after school, "I must learn to concentrate my mind on my work in school."

I learned early in life it was good to choose good companions. I noticed how decent fellows got into trouble following the wrong crowd and suffering the consequences.

After I became a Christian, I learned that the Word of God - the Bible, was food for my soul and a light on my pathway through life. I haven't missed many days when I did not read a chapter from the Bible. A verse of a song goes like this:

The Bible stands like a rock undaunted
'Mid the raging storms of time;
Its pages burn with the truth eternal,
And they glow with a light sublime.
The Bible stands though the hills may tumble
It will firmly stand when the earth shall crumble;
I will plant my feet on its firm foundation,
For the Bible stands.
Haldor Lilenas, 1917

"The Word of our God shall stand forever."
Isaiah 40:8

I have learned in life to cultivate good habits which are now paying off later in life. I did not abuse my body by smoking or drinking alcohol. I never tasted beer. On the farm I worked hard: clearing land, caring for sheep, shearing sheep, milking cows, etc. Good eating habits, good sleeping habits, and good daily exercise; I have learnt these contribute to good health. There is a saying, "You are what you eat." I seldom indulged in eating junk foods or drinking soda drinks. I ate good food such as plenty of fruit and vegetables and seldom ate in between meals. I was hardly ever sick and I am so grateful for good health.

A lesson I learned in Bible School in Melbourne was to begin each day right. All students were required to get up at 6 am and from 6:30 to 7:30 we practised "quiet time" which meant personal devotions, alone with God. After I graduated, I kept up this valuable practice and have enjoyed it all through the years.

I have enjoyed reading good books and missionary magazines, learning a lot from those who were further along the road than I was. When in candidate training for the mission field, reading certain missionary biographies was required of us.

I learned to trust God's Holy Spirit in me to accomplish what I couldn't naturally do myself. He enabled me to not only learn three foreign languages (*French, Swahili, Bangala*) but also to preach and teach fluently in them. I learned that Christ in me was adequate for every situation I had to face. He gave discernment as to how to act in a crisis and to make right decisions. I didn't have to lean on my own understanding.

Epilogue, 1989 to 1992

Aubrey stopped adding to his memoir at the end of 1989 and passed away in April of 1992 at the age of eighty. A few things of note did happen in those two years that should be mentioned here to make his story complete.

In mid-1990 his daughter Carol, had started feeling ill at Yamoussoukro Bible Institute where she and Jim were teaching in Ivory Coast. A French doctor diagnosed her as having leukaemia on July 12 and advised her to go home immediately for treatment. Hulda had just arrived in Abidjan for a visit with the family and Jim told her the news when he picked her up at the airport. She stayed overnight and accompanied Carol back to Canada the next day. Carol's brothers met her at the airport in Calgary with an ambulance and she was taken to Foothills Hospital. In the early morning of July 31, Carol died of an unknown infection after chemotherapy was started and depleted her infection-fighting white blood cells. It was a tremendous shock for all of us. Jim and the children, who had to wait in Africa while things were sold and packed up, just made it home in time to be with her a little while. She was laid to rest in Three Hills in early August.

Aubrey was diagnosed with prostate cancer and had surgery in 1991. He recovered slowly and was able to continue his regular walks down to the Three Hills Post Office in the centre of town. He was reading less, as he said he couldn't concentrate for long. He planted less vegetables in the garden and we all noticed he was slowing down. Aubrey however, still

thrived on visits from his children and grandchildren and up-
held them all in prayer daily.

On Easter Sunday, April 1992, many of the family were
gathered at Aubrey and Hulda's home in Three Hills for Easter
dinner. Aubrey had just taken the smaller grandchildren to a
nearby playground. Upon his return he came into the living
room and had a cup of tea. Then as we all carried on with our
conversations, he slipped away. Despite immediate CPR and
an ambulance ride over to the nearby hospital, Aubrey was
already gone, having suffered a major heart attack.

There is a long, straight road that leads west out of the
town of Three Hills. It passes a small cemetery surrounded by
tall pine trees that provide a natural and stately vertical border
separating the grave stones from the wheat fields that stretch
to the horizon in three directions. If you happen to visit when
the sun is setting, a gentle prairie breeze might nudge the tops
of the stately evergreen sentinels and their movement will
draw your eye to the spiny silhouette of the Rocky Mountains.
We buried Aubrey there beside his daughter. His long journey
complete, his soul already rejoicing as the long road disap-
peared over the horizon.

AUBREY BROWN, 1986

Many audio and visual details such as maps, photographs, audio recordings and a family tree can be found in the blog version of this book.

aubreysbistro.wordpress.com

www.ingramcontent.com/pod-product-compliance
Lightning Source LLC
LaVergne TN
LVHW091252080426
835510LV00007B/223